Design a portfolio that will make you stand out in interviewing

Take the guesswork out of deciding what to include in your portfolio

Create your portfolio quickly, using the easy-to-follow, step-by-step instructions

Develop a fail-proof way to transfer your portfolio to others

create your
DIGITAL
portfolio

The Fast Track to Career Success

SUSAN AMIRIAN, Ed.D.
ELEANOR FLANIGAN, Ed.D.

JIST Works
America's Career Publisher

Create Your Digital Portfolio
The Fast Track to Career Success

© 2006 by Susan Amirian and Eleanor Flanigan

Published by JIST Works, an imprint of JIST Publishing, Inc.

8902 Otis Avenue

Indianapolis, IN 46216-1033

Phone: 1-800-648-JIST   Fax: 1-800-JIST-FAX

E-mail: info@jist.com   Web site: www.jist.com

Support material for instructors using this book in the courses they teach is available. The *Create Your Digital Portfolio Instructor's Resources CD-ROM* (ISBN 1-59357-255-7) contains additional examples of portfolios, PowerPoint slides, test questions, and more. Call 1-800-648-JIST for details.

Quantity discounts are available for JIST products. Please call 1-800-648-JIST or visit www.jist.com for a free catalog and more information.

Visit www.jist.com for information on JIST, free job search information, book excerpts, and ordering information on our many products. For free information on 14,000 job titles, visit www.CAREEROINK.com.

Acquisitions Editor: Barb Terry

Development Editor: Jennifer Eberhardt

Cover and Interior Designer: Aleata Howard

Interior Layout: Marie Kristine Parial-Leonardo

Proofreader: Linda Seifert

Indexer: Cheryl Lenser

Printed in Canada

10 09 08 07 06 05   9 8 7 6 5 4 3 2 1

ISBN 1-59357-254-9

ABOUT THIS BOOK

Create Your Digital Portfolio takes the mystery out of creating a portfolio that will impress anyone who views it. The authors use clearly written "Step by Step" sections and easy-to-follow worksheets to quickly unveil each facet of creating a digital portfolio in the PDF format. This book guides you through collecting and organizing the items that will go into your portfolio, converting nonelectronic items to electronic format, and creating and distributing your portfolio.

You will enjoy using this highly illustrated book. Its sample portfolios and screen shots show you how to work with Adobe Acrobat software.

About the Authors

Dr. Susan Amirian is Assistant Professor in the Department of Media Communications and Technology at East Stroudsburg University in Pennsylvania. Her methods of teaching students how to create portfolios has been showcased on the Adobe Web site.

Dr. Eleanor Flanigan is Professor of Information and Decision Sciences in the School of Business at Montclair University in New Jersey.

Acknowledgements from Susan Amirian

I would like to thank my co-author, Eleanor Flanigan, for her enthusiasm, encouragement, and wonderful talents in creating this book with me.

Thanks also to our editor Jennifer Eberhardt for her tremendous insight, suggestions, patience, and vision in completing this giant task of creating a book and teacher's guide.

I am very grateful to the people at JIST for understanding and encouraging the vision of a guide for creating portfolios using Adobe Acrobat. Thank you to Barb Terry for creating the path and the team that brought this book to life.

I would like to also acknowledge the people who have yielded in my personal life to allow me the time and concentration to create this book. My son, Garen, has been my greatest support and encouragement in all of my endeavors. My co-workers Gary Braman, Terry Giffel, and

Elzar Camper listened patiently, offered suggestions and support, and helped me when I had too much on my plate. Thank you to my Dean, Sam Hausfather, who always enthusiastically supports my exploration with technologies for teaching and learning.

Acknowledgements from Eleanor Flanigan

This book was born in the creative mind of my co-author Susan Amirian, a woman with imagination, vision, patience, knowledge, and practicality. It has been a pleasure to collaborate with her to bring this work to fruition. Along with Susan, I thank the editors and publication group at JIST for the opportunity to work with them.

Because no endeavor of this kind is done without a backup team, I would like to express my gratitude to those who gave me encouragement and support—my husband, Dr. John Elias, my two daughters, Rebecca and Rachel, and my many friends who asked all the right questions.

Reviewers

Steve Adler
Learning Systems Integrator
Office of Curriculum and Instruction
Northern Valley Regional High School
  District
Demarest, New Jersey

Risa Blair
Teacher
Pine Crest School

Arlene C. Borthwick, Ph.D.
Associate Professor, Technology
  in Education
National-Louis University
Chicago, Illinois

Bettye Finnel
Executive Director
Grayson County Juvenile Alternatives
Sherman, Texas

Ali Hanyaloglu
Adobe Systems

Becky McKnight, P.T., M.S.
Program Coordinator
Physical Therapist Assistant Program
Ozarks Technical Community College

TABLE OF CONTENTS

Who Needs a Portfolio?

In This Chapter

- Learn what a portfolio is
- Explore why you need a portfolio
- Understand the advantages of a digital portfolio
- See why Acrobat is the best software for creating a portfolio

You've probably picked up this book because you want answers to questions that you have about creating a portfolio. With that in mind, this chapter asks and answers the most common questions people have when they start putting together a portfolio. Let's begin with the first and most obvious question: What is a portfolio?

What Is a Portfolio?

A *portfolio* is a method of collecting artifacts to distribute or present. In the past, the only people who created portfolios were artists and designers, but that is no longer true. Today, people in all types of jobs use portfolios. Anyone who does work that they want to show to others should consider creating a portfolio. Figures 1.1 and 1.2 show examples of pages from portfolios created by students just like you.

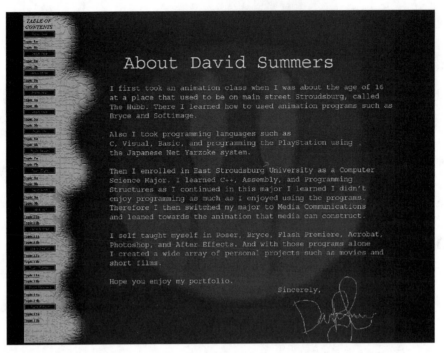

1.1 A page from a portfolio created by David Summers.

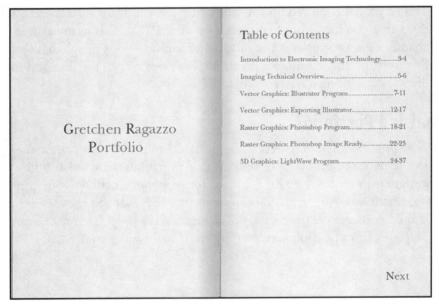

1.2 A page from a portfolio created by Gretchen Ragazzo.

Why Do I Need a Portfolio?

Sometimes you create a portfolio with a specific goal in mind, such as when you are applying to a university, looking for a new job, or asking for a promotion. Often, opportunities come up unexpectedly, and if you can quickly demonstrate your skills and qualifications, you will be in a good position to benefit. These opportunities can happen at school, in the office, at a conference, on a train, at a party, or through a friend. Think about how much more effective it would be to hand someone a portfolio of your work instead of a just a resume or business card.

Take a moment to think about the different kinds of work you do and why you might need to show examples of your work in an organized and efficient way to someone else. You could:

- Use your portfolio for job hunting. The portfolio could be part of your introduction at a meeting or presentation.

- Collect documentation of the job you do to show to your manager. This proof could be useful when it comes time for you to be promoted or to justify why your company should keep you as an employee.

- Collect papers or other items from a course you are taking to demonstrate your understanding and to show completion of the course requirements. You could also submit a portfolio to your teacher for grading.

- Show your portfolio to your employer to get reimbursement for a class you've taken or to demonstrate skills or requirements needed for certification. (*Certification* is a formal statement that a person has demonstrated certain levels of performance for certain skills or tasks.) For example, anyone wanting to become a doctor or lawyer must be approved by the state in which they will practice. A portfolio can demonstrate that a person has met the specific requirements of that state.

Why Create a *Digital* Portfolio?

For many years, the tradition in visual arts was to haul portfolios to clients for presentation (see Figure 1.3). Most portfolios were zippered, buckled, and latched. They were folders, boxes, books, and binders. The nice ones were leather. Many came in business-like shades of brown or black. And some of them were really big.

1.3 Traditional portfolios were difficult to copy and update.

Inside, the work was mounted on boards or thick black paper, or the work was laminated. Special carriers held slides, transparencies, and video tapes. Binders held papers in plastic sleeves. The portfolios were heavy, hard to transport, and especially vulnerable to damage.

Avoid a Bad Experience

Here is the story of one job hunter's experience with her paper portfolio:

> One day as she rode the elevator up to an interview, the doors opened, and another woman carrying several cups of coffee tripped while getting onto the elevator. The job hunter carefully wiped the spill off of the exterior of her portfolio, but it wasn't until she began her interview that she opened the portfolio and saw that coffee had run down each page.

> Needless to say, this job applicant didn't get the job. More importantly, she had to collect new copies of all of her work, mount them, and re-create her portfolio because all of her work was all based on hard copies (printouts or other non-digital work).

Although some people still prefer traditional portfolios, digital portfolios are quickly becoming the new standard for delivering resumes and work samples. Digital portfolios have many advantages. Digital portfolios can be

- Portable and easily duplicated.

- Left with a client or potential employer.

- Delivered in person, by e-mail, or through the Web.

- Password protected and secured so that the person viewing your work cannot copy or make changes to the portfolio.

- Produced so that the viewer doesn't need to have the original software you used to create a file in order to view it.

- Printed if the viewer prefers printed copies.

- Shown over and over again without showing signs of wear.

- Duplicated quickly if you need more than one copy or want a backup.

Digital portfolios have other advantages, as described in the following sections.

Demonstrate Your Skills in Different Ways

A paper portfolio or resume tells an employer about your skills and abilities. A digital portfolio, however, not only tells an employer about your qualities but *shows* your skills and abilities. By incorporating *multimedia* (using a combination of text, sound, video, graphics, or animation), you can present a video of yourself doing your job, making a speech, or documenting your success. Anyone who views your digital portfolio can look at your "pages" and at the same time hear your voice pointing out the highlights. Reading, seeing, hearing, and interacting with your digital portfolio adds another dimension to the reviewer's experience and is an extremely effective method of communication.

A digital portfolio also demonstrates your skill in producing a variety of effective, electronic documents. Whereas a paper resume can only describe your software skills, a digital portfolio provides a chance to *show* your software abilities and creativity.

Target Your Skills to a Specific Audience

After you create your portfolio, you can easily pull out, or *extract*, different pages to create special mini-portfolios that target the specific needs of a job or company. You can present any number of pages from your original portfolio—from one page to one hundred. For example, if your school counselor wants just a small sample of your work to keep on file or to e-mail to potential employers, you can create a smaller sample from your original portfolio.

Be Prepared

You never know when an opportunity might surface. Keep a copy of your portfolio on a USB flash drive, Zip disk, or CD so that you can show it to others. A *flash drive* is a small, portable drive that contains flash memory, which is a type of memory that can be erased and rewritten to. Flash drives are also called *thumb drives* or *jump drives*. A *Zip disk* is removable disk that stores files and is used with a Zip drive.

Today, many companies post job openings on the World Wide Web. These companies may post openings on their own Web site, or they may post openings to a job site such as Monster.com. People applying for these jobs then have the option to upload a resume or provide a link to a Web page of their work. Instead of sending just a resume, you can send an entire digital portfolio that provides work samples and evidence of your abilities. If you post to a Web site yourself, be sure to include a link to your portfolio so that potential employers have a chance to see your resume and work samples at the same time.

Why Should I Use Acrobat to Create a Digital Portfolio?

One of the first things you will need to think about as you begin the process of creating a digital portfolio is what format it will take. This book focuses on the format that we currently think is the best: the Portable Document Format (PDF).

In a recent article for *Communication Arts* magazine, Ellen Shapiro promoted the idea of using the PDF file format for a portfolio because it "can be e-mailed, printed out as a booklet and printed out in a larger presentation format for interviews. It is the delivery system for the 2000's: flexible and fast."

PDF is a way in which to save electronic documents so that the text, color, and imagery in the original document look the same to the person viewing the PDF. By using the free *Adobe Reader* software, anyone viewing the PDF can see a copy of the original document, regardless of which program you used to create the document. For example, if you create a resume in Adobe InDesign but the person to whom you're sending the resume can view only QuarkXPress files, you can create and send a PDF instead.

Using the PDF format for your electronic portfolio has many advantages:

- The PDF format is a business standard. This means that when you send your PDF portfolio for review, the chances are very good that the person reviewing your portfolio will be familiar with the format. That person will probably have Adobe Reader and will be able to open your document because PDF is a format he or she works with every day.

Adobe Reader Is Everywhere

Adobe, the maker of Adobe Reader, has distributed more than 500 million copies of this free program. This means that you are creating your portfolio in a format that potentially millions of people around the world could read.

- The PDF format is universal in that it comes in several different languages, is supported by different computer systems (such as Microsoft Windows and Apple Macintosh), and can be used with all popular Web browsers (such as Internet Explorer or Opera). The PDF format is used by governments as well as businesses throughout the world.

- Having the ability to work with and create PDFs will be attractive to your employer. Because PDF is a business standard, knowing how to work with PDFs to incorporate a broad range of document formats is a skill asset. Employers who move toward *paperless offices* (workplaces in which efforts are made to use digital files wherever possible in order to eliminate the use of paper from day-to-day work operations) value employees who also reflect that value in the management of their own paperwork.

- PDFs are independent of the software or computer system that created the original document. This means that you could create your digital portfolio by using Microsoft Word on a Macintosh computer and someone who uses a Windows computer would still be able to view your file, exactly as you intended.

- PDFs maintain the same formatting found in your original document. Examples of formatting include page margins or typefaces. A *typeface* is a set of letters and numbers that are designed to have a similar slant and thickness.

Why This Book Uses Acrobat Professional

As previously mentioned, anyone can view a PDF by using the free Adobe Reader program. To create a PDF, however, you need to use a version of *Adobe Acrobat*. Although Adobe offers different versions of its Acrobat software, in this book, we will use Adobe Acrobat Professional. Acrobat Professional has the broadest capability for containing, displaying, and converting a variety of *media* (such as text, sound, video, or animation) into digital portfolios.

PDF portfolios are easy to archive, update, and customize. When you *archive* files, you are storing them in an organized way so that you can easily locate and retrieve them.

Note

For more information about Acrobat, visit www.adobe.com.

The PDF format also allows greater flexibility in adapting your portfolio contents to construct focused mini-portfolios. In the next chapter, you will organize a collection of all of the possible items for your portfolio. You will then use these items to create a *master portfolio* that contains every personal characteristic and demonstration of knowledge, skills, achievement, and recognition you can think of. By using the PDF format, you can modify different pieces of your master portfolio to create a presentation targeted to specific employers, jobs, or presentations.

In This Chapter

In this chapter, you learned what a portfolio is and why having one is important. You also explored the advantages of having a digital portfolio (instead of having a traditional portfolio) and learned why using Adobe Acrobat Professional software is one of the best ways to create a digital portfolio.

1.1 Idea Starters

Directions: Take a moment to reflect on the following questions and then write an answer to each.

1. How do you imagine that a digital portfolio could be useful to you in your career plans?

   _____

   _____

2. Where might you go to find examples of digital portfolios that others have created?

   _____

   _____

3. What aspects of digital portfolios appeal to you most? What aspects appeal to you least?

   _____

   _____

(continued)

(continued)

1.1 Idea Starters

4. How do you currently collect and display items related to your career (paper or digital)?

_____

_____

5. What are some of the items you might want to include in your digital portfolio?

_____

_____

Collect and Organize Items for Your Portfolio

In This Chapter

- Find out what kinds of items people include in portfolios
- Identify items to include in your portfolio
- Collect items for your portfolio and determine how to store them
- Organize items you will use in your portfolio

Now that you understand what a portfolio is, it's time to start gathering items to put into your portfolio. In the beginning, it may seem as if it takes a lot of time and effort to prepare your items for a digital portfolio. And the prep work does take a lot of time. The payoff, however, is worth the time you put into it. For example, if you get a call to show your portfolio but your only copy is already out for review, you might lose a job opportunity because you have nothing to show. With a digital portfolio, however, you quickly create and deliver another copy.

What Do People Put in a Portfolio?

Whether you're putting together a portfolio for classroom use or to send to potential employers, your digital portfolio will contain a lot of different items. Because the reasons for creating a portfolio vary and because the types of work we each do varies, the kinds of items that you will collect and display in a portfolio depends on the kinds of items you produce and why you need to show them (see Figure 2.1). Your portfolio could contain art, photography, text documents, Web pages, presentations, performance videos, certificates of achievement, spreadsheets, calendars, schedules, reports, and more. These various items are known as *artifacts*.

2.1 Just about any item that demonstrates a success can be put into your digital portfolio.

The following list describes some of the people who create portfolios, their reasons for creating them, and the types of items they include.

- **Students** might create a portfolio for their classes to demonstrate what they learned (see Figure 2.2) or to get an internship or employment.

2.2 This page, from the portfolio of Pat Wiencek, shows a class assignment.

- **Teachers** might create a portfolio of their course work and professional development for their job review or promotion. Teachers might also use a portfolio for *tenure*, which is a guarantee that their position will be held permanently. Figure 2.3 shows an example of such a portfolio.

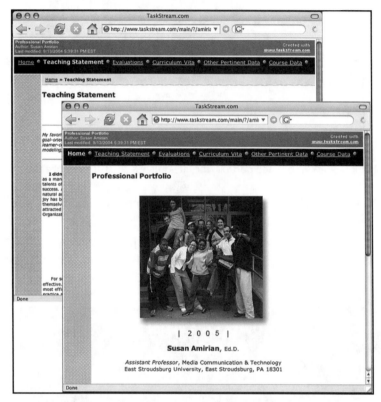

2.3 An example of a teacher's portfolio, in which typical elements might include a teaching statement or examples of lesson plans.

- **Artists** collect their work in portfolios, as shown in Figure 2.4, to seek full-time or freelance employment or to obtain gallery showings or private commissions. A *private commission* is when an artist is hired and paid to produce a creative work for an individual or company.

- **Sales people** create portfolios of their products in order to demonstrate their track record of success, awards and recognition, and ways of working with new clients.

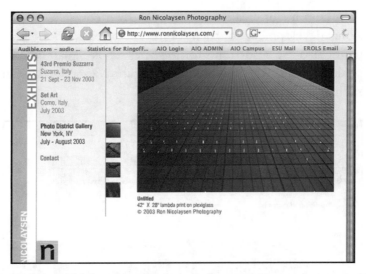

2.4 This photographer's Web-based portfolio includes images, artist statements, and a biography.

- **Office workers** collect data and documents to demonstrate their productivity, creativity and work ethic for *retention* (a performance assessment that depends on whether a person will keep their job), promotion, and performance reviews. An example of a page that demonstrates professional work is shown in Figure 2.5.

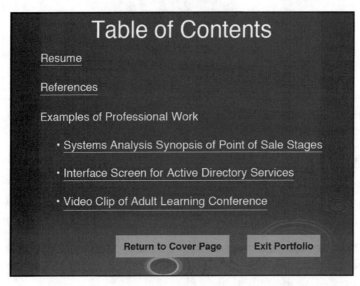

2.5 This example from the PowerPoint portion of a digital portfolio provides examples of professional work.

- **Craftsmen**, such as painters or landscapers, create portfolios that showcase their skills and experience and that demonstrate *proficiencies* (skills at which a high level of ability has been achieved) and certifications. This helps them find new clients or get promotions.

- **IT (Information Technology) workers**, such as computer programmers, show systems they have designed and include proof of certifications.

- **Customer service representatives** show how they solve problems, provide data on their effectiveness, and showcase letters from customers expressing their satisfaction.

Now that you've seen a few examples of portfolios, the next section helps you to determine the types of items that will be useful to include in your own portfolio.

What Should I Include in My Portfolio?

Quite simply, your portfolio is a way to show your best work, demonstrate your skills, and present your experience and interests in order to give others a clear understanding of your qualifications for a job, a promotion, or advancement.

A portfolio can also be used as a tool to assess your personal and professional skills and goals. By organizing your work, you are better able to understand your own skills, strengths, and weaknesses. Your portfolio can point you to areas in which you might want to improve as well as suggest a change in careers.

Take a moment to think about the parts of your life, both professional and personal, which would be important to save in a portfolio. Figure 2.6 shows how to categorize those various parts of your life by using the acronym STEPPER.

By reflecting on each of these categories and filling them in with words that describe your own experiences and accomplishments, you will have the material you need to create your career portfolio. Although the various categories might contain personal items, keep in mind that you are putting together a career portfolio for professional use. Sometimes personal interests and accomplishments are appropriate; sometimes they are not.

S	Skills (Summary of qualifications or experience)
T	Technical ability, Teamwork, Tutoring, Talents
E	Education (Degrees, certification, courses)
P	Professional awards (Honors, leadership, associations)
P	Personal info (Honors, hobbies, sports interest or achievement, clubs)
E	Employment history and Experience with volunteering
R	Resume, References, Resources

2.6 Use STEPPER to break down the various parts of your personal and professional life.

For example, if you were applying for a position with a travel agency, your personal experience (Personal info category) with a hobby such as skiing would support your ability to lead tours to the Swiss Alps. Another example might be your love of camping. To make this relevant to your career portfolio, you could relate your camping experience (Personal info category) with volunteering with youth groups (Experience with volunteering). These items would enrich your career portfolio if you were interested in a career as a forest ranger or in marketing for an outdoor clothing company.

Types of Information to Include in Your Portfolio

As you begin building your master portfolio, you should create a list of your personal characteristics, anything that demonstrates your knowledge, experience, and skills, and any other achievements you can think of. Later, you can select and edit the contents of your master portfolio to create *targeted mini-portfolios*, which are based on a specific career goal or purpose.

Think about the story you want to tell about yourself through your portfolio. Begin by deciding which information you want to share about yourself in your portfolio. You can break down this information into five categories:

- Personal
- Education
- Career
- Accomplishments
- Abilities

Table 2.1 includes some ideas for the types of information you might want to include for each of these categories.

Table 2.1 Types of Information to Include in a Portfolio

PERSONAL

Personal Information	Your name, mailing address, telephone number, and e-mail address.
Home Page	Web site home pages.
Personal Interests	Hobbies, skills not directly related to your job, participation in sports, consulting, volunteer work, memberships, and leadership roles in any of these areas.
Personality Inventories	Tests that you have taken, such as Myers-Briggs, that demonstrate your personality type and career types that match with that personality.
Permits	Licenses, passports, or visas that allow you to work in specific careers, such as truck driving or nursing, or in geographic locations, such as Asia.
Military Service	Dates and type of service, honors, promotions, and rank achieved.
Activities	Sports, clubs, memberships, or other personal activities.
Role Models	People whom you have admired or those who have led you to make your career choices.
Mentors	People who have supported or advised you in the development of your career. If these people are willing to serve as a reference for you, include their mailing address, telephone number, and e-mail address.

EDUCATION

Education History	Include the school attended, dates of attendance, degrees earned, relevant courses, and any special papers, theses, exams, or certifications. Could begin with high school or undergraduate education.
Transcripts	Official transcripts of all degree programs, courses toward certification, and exam results.
Professional Development	Continuing educational experiences, workshops, or training you have had to keep your skills up-to-date.
Licenses	Professional licenses or certifications earned.
Languages	Ability to speak or write in other languages.

(continued)

(continued)

Table 2.1 Types of Information to Include in a Portfolio

CAREER	
Experience	For each job held, include the position title, organization name, supervisor, address, dates of employment, and description of job duties and special accomplishments.
Resume	A downloadable, digital resume.
Teamwork	Demonstration that you are able to work as part of a team. Include project descriptions or evaluations from team members or leaders.
Management	Examples of work experiences that demonstrate your ability to manage projects and people.
Evaluations	Career reviews conducted by advisors, counselors, and employers.
Professional Practice	Publications, presentations of research, or career successes.
Recognition	Honors, awards, and achievements received for work. Include dates and descriptions of the recognition.
Career Plan	Goals and objectives for the future. Include an action plan, timeline, and a personal mission statement.
References	Letters of reference from employers. Include names, mailing addresses, telephone numbers, and e-mail addresses.
ACCOMPLISHMENTS	
Products	Pictures and descriptions of your projects.
Letters	Items related to your accomplishment of specific tasks or for a job well done.
News	Stories about you published in company, local, or national media such as newspapers, newsletters, or Web sites.
ABILITIES	
Skills	Communication skills, project management skills, writing skills, demonstration of ability to work with diverse groups, software skills, or any specialized skills for your career area.

Now that you've had a chance to review the items in Table 2.1, it's time to start creating a list of your own accomplishments and skills. You can use the following worksheet as a guide. Although you may think some items aren't completely relevant or you may decide not to include each item in your portfolio, the bigger your list is to choose from, the better. Remember to think about the story you want to tell.

2.1 Creating an Information Sheet

Directions: For each category, list as many pieces of information about yourself as you can think of. After you are finished, share this worksheet with people who know you and ask them if they can think of any items you might have forgotten.

Personal

_____

_____

Education

_____

_____

Career

_____

_____

Accomplishments

_____

_____

Abilities

_____

_____

This worksheet is a guide to get you started. Your final list may be several pages long. As you accomplish new things, be sure to come back and add them to this worksheet so that it is always up-to-date. Then, refer to this worksheet as you begin pulling together the various items for your portfolio.

Collecting Items and Organizing Them

As you build your portfolio, you will find that you have an overwhelming amount of information. For this reason, from the very beginning, it is important to set up a method of organizing this information. In this section, you will set up an organizational strategy that includes how and where to store the items you want to include in your portfolio. This section also includes a suggestion for naming and organizing the files so that your files are easy to locate. The last thing you want to do is to open and close a hundred or more files to find out what is in them. A good naming convention will make building and updating your portfolio easy.

Save and Store Your Original Items

You might have several kinds of items: paper (such as a school transcript), three-dimensional objects (such as a package design mock-up), digital documents (such as a PowerPoint presentation), or *analog tapes* (a non-digital format such as a VHS video tape or a cassette tape).

Because you are creating a digital portfolio, you will need to convert your paper documents, three-dimensional objects, and analog tapes into a digital format. Then, you will want to save both forms of the item—the original file (or object) and the new digital file. Table 2.2 provides descriptions for various storage options.

Table 2.2 Ways to Store Items for Your Portfolio	
STORAGE TYPE	**DESCRIPTION**
PAPER, 3-DIMENSIONAL OBJECTS AND TAPES File boxes or filing cabinets	**FOR PHYSICAL OBJECTS, IT IS EASIEST TO WORK WITH THEM OVER TIME IF THE ARE ALL IN THE SAME PLACE.** Set aside a special place to gather your non-digital artifacts as you collect them. Then, store them together in a filing cabinet, or use file folders or boxes designed just for this purpose.

STORAGE TYPE	DESCRIPTION
DIGITAL FILES Computer hard drive	**FOR DIGITAL DOCUMENTS, YOU WILL NEED TO DECIDE HOW YOU WILL STORE ALL COPIES OF YOUR DIGITAL FILES.** If your computer has enough hard disk space available, then you can simply create a folder on your desktop to organize and store your portfolio artifacts. If your computer space is limited or if you are working in a lab or on public computer where you do not have storage space, you can use any of the following options.
External hard drive 30 GB – 1 TB	An *external hard drive* is a type of computer hardware that connects to your computer and works similarly to your hard drive. Often, these drives are portable and come with a broad range of storage capacities. Look for either USB2 or Firewire ports so that data can travel as quickly as possible between the computer you are working on and the external hard drive.
USB flash drive 128 MB – 4 GB	Flash drives (also called *thumb drives* or *jump drives*) are a good way to transport files between computers. They might also be a good storage media for your digital portfolio and artifacts, but it depends of the number and size of your files.
CD / DVD 650 MB – 700 MB	Both CDs and DVDs are reliable and economical ways to store digital items. You may have to use multiple CDs to store your files, but because of the small expense, you can also make backups economically. Rewritable CDs will let you add files to your discs over time. Be sure to label and store your discs in a box with slipcovers or in a case.
Zip disk 100 MB – 750 MB	Zip disks are available in several storage capacities, and you must have the right capacity for the Zip drive you are using. Although Zip disks are an acceptable method of saving your work, the number of people who still have and use Zip drives is getting smaller.
Floppy disk 1.4 MB	Floppy disks are not recommended because they have limited storage capacity and because many new computers no longer have floppy drives. If you have original items on floppy disks, consider copying them to your hard drive or the storage device on which you are creating and saving your portfolio.

A Bit of This, a Byte of That

Here's how all of those bytes add up:

Megabyte (MB)   1,000,000 bytes.

Gigabyte (GB)   1024 Megabytes. Also used to refer to 1000 Megabytes.

Terabyte (TB)   1024 Gigabytes. Also used to refer to 1000 Gigabytes.

After you determine the storage method that is best for you, you can begin setting up electronic folders to organize your files.

Set Up Your Folder Structure

After you choose a storage method but before you assemble any digital files, you need to set up a folder structure on your computer (or other storage device) so that you can more easily store and organize your files. By using a consistent structure from the very start, you will be able to more easily retrieve and distribute your portfolio when the time comes.

Throughout this book, we will refer to the folder structure shown here. Also, we will tell you where to put each of the files you create as you collect your artifacts and build your portfolio. Be sure to name and place files exactly as shown and described in the following steps because this structure will guide your work throughout the rest of the process.

Step by Step

1. Create a new folder on your computer (or the storage device you are using) and name it **Portfolio Files**.

2. Within this folder, create four subfolders and name them as follows:

   Attached Files
   Multimedia
   PDFs
   Portfolio Artifacts

   Your folder structure should now match the one shown in Figure 2.7.

2.7 By using the folder structure shown here, you can easily store and organize your files. (The folders are shown here in List view on a Windows computer).

Create a List of Artifacts

Now that you have thought about what you want to include in your portfolio and you have set up your electronic folders, the next step is to create a list of all the items as you collect them. The reason you are creating a list is so that you can easily locate and organize your portfolio without having to go back and search through your box full of items. Instead, you can just search through your list.

Step by Step

1. Make sure that all the things you want to include in your portfolio are in one place and that you have easy access to them.

2. Make sure that you completed the "Creating an Information Sheet" worksheet found earlier in this chapter.

3. By using a word-processing program such as Microsoft Word, complete Worksheet 2.2, "Creating a List of Portfolio Items." You will fill in one row for each of your portfolio items. For each item, you need to include information for each of the following:

Number: Starting at number *001*, assign a different number to each item. (If you think you will have more than 999 items, start numbering at *0001* instead.)

Category: Using the categories from Table 2.1, fill in either *Personal*, *Education*, *Career*, *Accomplishments*, or *Abilities*.

Brief Description: Write a brief description of each item.

Type: List the type of item the original is, such as a Word file, video, or hard copy. *Hard copy* typically referes to a printout of an electronic document.

Format: List the form the original is in, such as paper (if it is a hard copy), video tape, or file extension (if it is a digital file).

When finished, your list will look similar to the one shown in Figure 2.8.

NUMBER	CATEGORY	BRIEF DESCRIPTION	TYPE OF ITEM	FORMAT
001	Career	Resume	Microsoft Word document	DOC
002	Career	Data system design	Microsoft Excel document	XLS
003	Education	Term project report on women in the military	Microsoft Word document	DOC
004	Education	Report for Art History	Microsoft Word document	DOC
005	Personal	Head shot, business attire	Studio photo	JPEG
006	Career	Promotional package product	Photo of the package	JPEG
007	Education	Term presentation for Art History	PowerPoint presentation	PPT
008	Education	Video of me giving the Art History presentation	Video tape	VHS
009	Career	Newsletter	Microsoft Word document	DOC
010	Personal	My home page	Web page	HTML
011	Education	My diploma	Paper document	Paper

2.8 A completed list of portfolio items. In this example worksheet, item number 001 is a resume that was created in Microsoft Word and saved with the .DOC format and file extension. The resume belongs to the Career category described in Table 2.1.

4. Save your list. Use a name that makes sense and save your list in a location so that you can easily find it later.

5. If you have not already done so, collect your items in a box. Alternatively, if you have several paper documents, use file folders. You will need to label each of your items.

6. Grab a pencil, and either directly on the document or on a sticky note, write the number you gave each item in your list on the actual items (use the "Creating a List of Portfolio Items" worksheet to do this). If you also have electronic files, proceed with the next step.

7. Make copies of all of your original digital files. Rename each of them so that each item includes the number and name that you assigned to them.

8. Save the copies of your newly named digital files into the Portfolio Artifacts folder that you created on your computer. Recall that this folder is found within the Portfolio Files folder.

2.2 Creating a List of Portfolio Items

Directions: Use the directions in the preceding Step by Step section to create an electronic version of the following table. Use a different row for each item you want to include in your portfolio.

NUMBER	CATEGORY	DESCRIPTION	TYPE	FORMAT
001				
002				
003				
004				
005				
006				
007				
008				
009				
010				

After you complete the preceding Step by Step section and the "Creating a List of Portfolio Items" worksheet, the next step is to sort your items by category. Doing this will group all of the items for each category, which you will use in the next chapter to create your resume. To perform a sort in Microsoft Word, follow these steps:

Step by Step

1. Open your list of portfolio items, if it is not already open.

2. Click anywhere in the table, and then go to Table > Select > Table to select the entire table.

3. With the table still selected, go to Table > Sort.

4. In the Sort dialog box, select Category from the drop-down menu and be sure the Ascending option is selected, as shown in Figure 2.9. Under the section My list has, click to select the Header row option button.

2.9 Use the Sort dialog box to arrange your items by category.

5. Click OK. Microsoft Word sorts your table with all items in each category grouped together (see Figure 2.10).

NUMBER	CATEGORY	BRIEF DESCRIPTION	TYPE OF ITEM	FORMAT
001	Career	Resume	Microsoft Word document	DOC
002	Career	Data system design	Microsoft Excel document	XLS
006	Career	Promotional package product	Photo of the package	JPEG
009	Career	Newsletter	Microsoft Word document	DOC
003	Education	Term project report on women in the military	Microsoft Word document	DOC
004	Education	Report for Art History	Microsoft Word document	DOC
007	Education	Term presentation for Art History	PowerPoint presentation	PPT
008	Education	Video of me giving the Art History presentation	Video tape	VHS
011	Education	My diploma	Paper document	Paper
012	Education	My transcript	Paper document	Papter
013	Education	Business course term paper	Microsoft Word document	DOC
005	Personal	Head shot, business attire	Studio photo	JPEG
010	Personal	My home page	Web page	HTML

2.10 A list of portfolio items, sorted by category.

6. Save your work.

You have now completed the prep work and are ready to begin creating your resume and portfolio.

In This Chapter

In this chapter, you explored the kinds of items people include in portfolios and began identifying the items you wanted to include in your own portfolio. You also collected your portfolio items, determined the best way to store them, and used a worksheet to organize all of the items you plan to use in your portfolio.

2.3 Idea Starters

Directions: Take a moment to reflect on the following questions and then write an answer to each.

1. With your particular skills and career goals, what are the advantages of a digital portfolio?

_____

_____

2. With your particular skills and career goals, what are the disadvantages of a digital portfolio?

_____

_____

3. Can you imagine a situation in which you would want to have your portfolio and resume on paper?

_____

_____

4. Can you imagine a situation in which you would want to have your portfolio and resume in digital form?

_____

_____

5. What is your plan for saving your digital files?

_____

_____

Create Your Resume and Storyboard

In This Chapter

- Create your resume
- Break down your resume for storyboarding purposes
- Create a storyboard to map out your portfolio

Up until now you have reflected upon and gathered your personal and career experiences. You categorized these along with your accomplishments and skills. Your portfolio items are now organized and sorted, so you are ready to combine the information into your portfolio. One document that helps to consolidate this information into an easily readable form is the resume.

Construct Your Resume

The first step in constructing your portfolio is to create your resume. A *resume* is a written summary of your education, skills, career objectives, and work experience. It is used primarily as a self-promotional tool for job hunting, job retention, or promotion.

In this chapter, you will use Microsoft Word to create a document that will become your resume. In addition to saving your resume in Microsoft Word format, you will save it as a plain text document that you can use to create and structure a PowerPoint presentation that will be part of your portfolio. Before you begin to work on your resume, however, you will need to:

- Make a copy of the "Creating an Information Sheet" and "Identifying Items for Your Portfolio" worksheets from Chapter 2. Place a copy of these worksheets beside your keyboard while you create your resume. Each of the five categories from the Information Sheet will match a section of your resume.

- Take a moment to review the example resumes shown in Figures 3.1 and 3.2, paying special attention to the formats and wording. You can use both of these resumes as a guide for constructing your own resume.

Checking Out Resume Samples

Both your local library and the Web have hundreds of examples of the various resume formats and styles available to you. Here are a few books that we recommend:

- *101 Best Tech Resumes* by Jay Block (McGraw-Hill)
- *Expert Resumes for Computer and Web Jobs* by Wendy Enelow and Louise Kursmark (JIST Works)
- *Best Resumes for College Students and New Grads: Jump-Start Your Career* by Louise Kursmark (JIST Works)
- *Resume Magic: Trade Secrets of a Professional Resume Writer* by Susan Whitcomb (JIST Works)

1777 Main Street.   Phone (555) 555-5555
Somewhere, ST 55555   E-mail Name1@hotmail.com

First Name Last Name

Objective

To obtain a position in International Finance using computer and analytic skills.

Summary of Software Programs/Languages

Microsoft Office2003 (Word, Excel, Access, PowerPoint, Outlook), Microsoft Publisher, MapPoint, Oracle, SAP, SQL, Visual Basic/VBA, Adobe Photoshop, Adobe Acrobat.

Education

MyUniversity   **MyUniversityTown, ST**

Bachelor of Science in Business Administration. (August 2006)

Dual majors: Management Information Systems and International Finance

Dean's List / GPA: 3.5/4.0

> Relevant Courses: Computer Applications; International Finance; Database Development; Operations Analysis; Networking; Systems Analysis and Design; Contemporary Issues in International Business

Employment

Store Supervisor / Sales Specialist

(May/04-Present)   Wireless Communications   Somewhere, ST

> Sell communication products and services through various locations.
> Distribute equipment; complete daily paperwork and inventory.
> Promote outside sales events.
> Selected as Top Sales Representative, Northeast Region.
> Designed in-store database and networked store computers

Head Server

(January/00-April/04)   The Local Restaurant   Wherever, ST

> Designed and updated weekly menu.
> Designed floor layouts for large group reservations (serving 70+ people).
> Interviewed and analyzed clients' needs for group parties
> Served as trouble-shooter and provided customer service.

Volunteer Activities

Represent School of Business on University Computer Committee.
Volunteer for hometown Red Cross Safe Rides Program.
Teach computer skills for hometown Adult School

Languages

Fluent in both oral and written Spanish

3.1 Resume Example #1.

First Name Last Name

12 Main Street	e-mail: name@hotmail.com
Somewhere, ST 07103	http://www.lastname.server.edu
555-555-5555	

Objective: To further the mission of a company in the field of information technology using my technical computer expertise along with my written and oral communication skills.

Education: Bachelor of Science   May 2006
My University Name, Somewhere, ST 22222
Major: Business Administration
Concentration: Management Information Systems
Cumulative GPA: 3.823/4.0; Dean's List (3 semesters)

Relevant Courses: Operations Analysis, Advanced Computer Applications, Networks in Business, Business Computer Programming, Database Development, Systems Analysis and Design, Contemporary Business Issues

Awards: School of Business Program Scholarship, Community Service Honor

Experience: ***Department of Career Services, MyUniversity***
Student Worker/Recruiter: Oct. 2004-Present
Recruit students for the Educational Opportunity Fund
Coordinate the structured tutoring program for students in conjunction with the University Learning Center
Assist in office: correspondence, phone duty, front desk interaction

Office of Residence Life, MyUniversity
Resident Assistant   Sept. 2005- Present
Responsible for 70 student residents directly and 350 residents indirectly
Serve as Head Assistant for team of 14 other resident assistants
Conduct student resident meetings
Arrange educational and recreational programs both on- and off-campus

ABC Home Loans Corporation, Somecity, ST
Summer Intern
Designed and maintained company database for field representatives.

Computer Skills: Microsoft Office 2003 (Word, Excel, Access, PowerPoint, Outlook), Microsoft Publisher, MapPoint, Oracle, SAP, SQL, Java, Visual Basic/VBA, Adobe Photoshop, Adobe Acrobat. MOUS certified.

Activities: ESL Program: Public Relations Committee; Treasurer, Alpha Zeta Fraternity; Editor, The Eagle, student newspaper; Vice-President, Latin American Student Association

Languages: Fluent in oral and written Spanish

3.2 Resume Example #2.

Step by Step

1. Start Microsoft Word (or a similar word-processing program).

2. Go to File > Page Setup. In the Page Setup dialog box, click the Paper tab and make sure that the Paper size is set to Letter. Then click the Margins tab and set the top, bottom, left, and right margins to 1 inch. Click OK.

3. Go to Format > Font and in the Font dialog box, choose a well-known typeface (such as Times New Roman or Arial) and choose a font size. The example resume shown in Figure 3.2 uses Times New Roman with 12-point font size. Click OK.

4. Now, while using the example resumes as a guide, fill in your own contact information. For example, fill in your name instead of the heading "First Name Last Name."

5. Type each of the categories shown in the left column of the example resumes. If a category does not pertain to you, you may wish to substitute the heading or remove it. However, remember that you will want to include information from each of the five categories included in the "Creating an Information Sheet" worksheet from Chapter 2.

6. For each category, add information about you—your objective, education, courses, skills, or awards. Refer to the "Identifying Items for Your Portfolio" worksheet that you completed in Chapter 2.

Resume Writing Tips

Keep the information you type concise but complete. Use verbs instead of full sentences to describe your employment duties and responsibilities or to describe volunteer activities.

7. Go to Tools > Spelling and Grammar. You can use this spell-checking feature to catch any mistakes or typographical errors in your resume.

8. Read your resume out loud to be sure you haven't repeated or missed any words.

9. Locate the list of portfolio items you created in Chapter 2 (from the worksheet "Creating a List of Portfolio Items"). Add your resume and then assign a number to it. Keep this number handy—you will use it in the next step to save your resume.

10. Go to File > Save and then in the Save dialog box, name the document with the artifact's number and the word "resume". Be sure to save your resume as a Microsoft Word document, which contains the *.doc* file extension. For example, your resume might be named 001-resume.doc. Before you click the Save button, navigate to the Portfolio Artifacts folder you created on your computer (or other storage device) in the previous chapter. Click Save. This document is your resume.

Tip

Show your resume to at least one other person who can give you honest, helpful feedback and who can also double-check for mistakes.

11. Go to File > Save As to save a copy of your resume. In the Save As dialog box, under Save as type, select Plain Text. This file name should be the same as the resume document, except the *.doc* file extension will change to *.txt* (such as 001-resume.txt) to indicate that you care creating a plain text file. Save this plain text version of your resume to your Portfolio Artifacts folder as well.

Why should you do this? Saving the document as text removes all formatting such as bold or tabs, as shown in Figure 3.3. You will use this plain document to copy and paste the text from your resume to a PowerPoint slide.

```
First Name Last Name
12 Main StreetSomewhere, ST 07103
e-mail: name@hotmail.com
http://www.lastname.server.edu
555-555-5555

Objective:
To further the mission of a company in the field of information technology
using my technical computer expertise along with my written and oral
communication skills.

Education:
Bachelor of Science, May 2006
My University Name, Somewhere, ST 22222
Major: Business Administration
Concentration: Management Information Systems
Cumulative GPA: 3.823/4.0; Dean's List (3 semesters)

Relevant Courses:
Operations Analysis
Advanced Computer Applications
Networks in Business
Business Computer Programming
Database Development
Systems Analysis and Design
Contemporary Business Issues

Awards:
School of Business Program Scholarship
Community Service Honor

Experience:
Department of Career Services, MyUniversity
Student Worker/Recruiter, Oct. 2004-Present
Recruit students for the Educational Opportunity Fund
Coordinate the structured tutoring program for students in conjunction with
the University Learning Center
Assist in office: correspondence, phone duty, front desk interaction

Office of Residence Life, MyUniversity
Resident Assistant, Sept. 2005- Present
Responsible for 70 student residents directly and 350 residents indirectly
Serve as Head Assistant for team of 14 other resident assistants
Conduct student resident meetings
Arrange educational and recreational programs both on- and off-campus

ABC Home Loans Corporation, Somecity, ST
Summer Intern
Designed and maintained company database for field representatives.

Computer Skills:
Microsoft Office 2003 (Word, Excel, Access, PowerPoint, Outlook)
Microsoft Publisher
MapPoint
```

3.3 Resume Example #2 saved as a plain text document.

Break Your Resume into Chunks

After your have prepared your resume document, the next step is to break it up into logical chunks so that you can present your information as individual pages, or *screens*, in your portfolio. Remember, you are designing a digital portfolio that will be presented primarily on a computer screen. Designing a presentation for the screen format differs from designing a document that will be printed out to paper in these two ways:

- A computer screen is a horizontal format, not vertical like a piece of paper.

- Most people don't like to read a lot of small type on a computer screen. Because of this you will use larger text and put less of it on each "page" (or screen) to make it easier to read.

To help you break the information in your resume into chunks, you will add horizontal lines, also known as *rules*. These lines will help you plan and give you a visual reminder that it is important to separate the various sections of your resume. You will use these to make your resume easier to read and also to set up your storyboards and PowerPoint slides. Figure 3.4 shows a resume that was created for this example.

```
First Name Last Name
12 Main StreetSomewhere, ST 07103
e-mail: name@hotmail.com
http://www.lastname.server.edu
555-555-5555
----------------------------------------------------------------------
Objective:
To further the mission of a company in the field of information technology
using my technical computer expertise along with my written and oral
communication skills.
----------------------------------------------------------------------
Education:
Bachelor of Science, May 2006
My University Name, Somewhere, ST 22222
Major: Business Administration
Concentration: Management Information Systems
Cumulative GPA: 3.823/4.0; Dean's List (3 semesters)

Relevant Courses:
Operations Analysis
Advanced Computer Applications
Networks in Business
Business Computer Programming
Database Development
Systems Analysis and Design
Contemporary Business Issues
----------------------------------------------------------------------
Awards:
School of Business Program Scholarship
Community Service Honor
----------------------------------------------------------------------
Experience:
Department of Career Services, MyUniversity
Student Worker/Recruiter, Oct. 2004-Present
Recruit students for the Educational Opportunity Fund
Coordinate the structured tutoring program for students in conjunction with
the University Learning Center
Assist in office: correspondence, phone duty, front desk interaction
----------------------------------------------------------------------
Office of Residence Life, MyUniversity
Resident Assistant, Sept. 2005- Present
Responsible for 70 student residents directly and 350 residents indirectly
Serve as Head Assistant for team of 14 other resident assistants
Conduct student resident meetings
Arrange educational and recreational programs both on- and off-campus
----------------------------------------------------------------------
ABC Home Loans Corporation, Somecity, ST
Summer Intern
Designed and maintained company database for field representatives.
----------------------------------------------------------------------
Computer Skills:
Microsoft Office 2003 (Word, Excel, Access, PowerPoint, Outlook)
Microsoft Publisher
MapPoint
```

3.4 Smaller chunks of information are easier to read and remember.

Step by Step

1. If the plain text version of your resume is not already open, go ahead and open it.

2. By using Figure 3.4 as an example, break the resume content into logical sections of information by using horizontal lines. You can create horizontal lines by typing dashes that separate the sections. If you have a printed copy, you can do this by using a ruler to draw the lines.

3. Because each chunk of information will be displayed on one page (or screen), take a moment to see how much content displays between each set of rules. Remember that your portfolio is a horizontal format. Your goal is to break up the information in a way that does not put too much type on any single page or screen.

4. Save your work.

Storyboard the Screens of Your Portfolio

After creating your resume and separating the sections into identifiable chunks, you will need to organize these chunks. You do this by creating a storyboard. A *storyboard* is a series of drawings that represent a process, or in this case a document—the portfolio. Storyboards are planning documents to help make sure that the steps you are taking make sense and to guide the creation of your portfolio.

Figure 3.5 shows a sample of a storyboard with several panels filled in. Each of these panels will later become individual slides in the PowerPoint presentation. Each panel, or "slide," contains the following items:

- A title that relates to the type of information being presented (such as Objective) or category (such as Education)

- A page number, in the lower-left corner

- Example text that will appear on the PowerPoint slide

- A description of the page's content

- A list of artifacts (portfolio items) and their names

For example, in Figure 3.5 you can see that panel #4, which relates to the Education category, has many relevant artifacts to support the information on that screen.

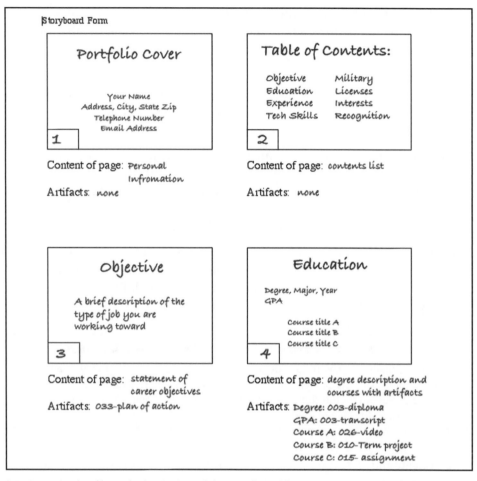

Storyboard Form

Portfolio Cover

Your Name
Address, City, State Zip
Telephone Number
Email Address

1

Content of page: Personal Infromation

Artifacts: none

Table of Contents:

Objective	Military
Education	Licenses
Experience	Interests
Tech Skills	Recognition

2

Content of page: contents list

Artifacts: none

Objective

A brief description of the type of job you are working toward

3

Content of page: statement of career objectives

Artifacts: 033-plan of action

Education

Degree, Major, Year
GPA

Course title A
Course title B
Course title C

4

Content of page: degree description and courses with artifacts

Artifacts: Degree: 003-diploma
GPA: 003-transcript
Course A: 026-video
Course B: 010-Term project
Course C: 015- assignment

3.5 An example of how the beginning of the storyboard for your resume might look.

Notice also that you can include information for introductory information. For example, Figure 3.5 shows a "cover" screen with your name and personal information. You can incorporate that information into a single screen as this storyboard does, or you can place the cover on the first screen and your personal information on the second screen.

Step by Step

1. On a piece of a paper, re-create the storyboard form. Make as many copies of the form as you need to contain all of the chunks of information from your resume.

2. You can work with a pencil or pen for this part of the process. Start by numbering each of the panels. Write the page number in the box at the lower left of each panel. This will be the order for your presentation.

3. In the first and second storyboard panels, which will be your port-folio "cover," fill in your name, mailing address, phone number, and e-mail address.

4. On the next panel, fill in your table of contents. The *table of contents* is a guide to the content that is included in your presentation. Your table of contents should match the category headings shown in the left column of your resume. Your table of contents will probably differ from the one shown on panel #2 in Figure 3.5.

5. For the remaining panels, fill in the content for each portfolio page. For each panel, indicate what that content is and include a descrip-tion of the content in the space below each panel. Do this for each chunk of information from your resume.

Setting Up Your Content for the Computer Screen

If you find that you are writing a lot and having to make the writing very small to fit in everything, consider breaking that information between two panels. Remember, you are designing for the computer screen and don't want to make the type so small that it is uncomfortable to read.

6. Locate the "Creating a List of Portfolio Items" worksheet you com-pleted in Chapter 2. Go back to the first panel and begin listing the corresponding artifacts below each panel.

Congratulations! You now have a resume and a plan for your portfolio. A big part of the creation of the portfolio is the gathering and organization of information and samples. In the next chapter, you will prepare your samples.

In This Chapter

In this chapter, you created your resume by using the information you collected in the previous chapter. You then broke down your resume into separate sections so that you could use them to create the storyboard for the PowerPoint presentation you will create. The storyboard contained both introductory information as well as a map of the pages that will become slides.

3.1 Idea Starters

Directions: Take a moment to reflect on the following questions and then write an honest answer to each.

1. Were there any pieces of your resume that were difficult to divide into chunks that would fit into a single screen? If so, what did you do to make them fit?

   _____

   _____

2. What type of content did you place on each screen of your storyboard?

   _____

   _____

3. Do you have additional content that you feel would be beneficial to include in your portfolio? If yes, please describe.

   _____

   _____

4. How is your storyboard similar to or different from those of your classmates?

   _____

   _____

5. Is there any content that you wanted to put in a different order but decided not to? Why or why not?

   _____

   _____

Build Your Portfolio Templates

In This Chapter

- Create PowerPoint slides from your storyboard
- Add a design theme to the PowerPoint presentation
- Choose and set up a method to navigate the PowerPoint presentation

Now that you have collected your portfolio items and created your resume, the next step is to construct the template for your master digital portfolio. Although there are many different ways to build a portfolio, we will use Microsoft PowerPoint in this book. PowerPoint makes it easy to produce professional-looking results, even if you have little or no experience in graphic design. Because PowerPoint comes with many design templates and themes, you can quickly create and view the format of your presentation on your computer screen.

What to Do If You're Using a Mac

The instructions and file extensions given in this chapter assume that you are using Microsoft PowerPoint for Windows. If you work on a Mac, you can use PowerPoint, Apple's Keynote, or any presentation software that you feel comfortable with.

Construct the Portfolio Template

The first step in building the digital portfolio document is to create a template and place the various categories of text from your resume on each slide. A *template* is a pattern or model used in the creation of many different kinds of things. There are clothing templates used for sewing, for instance. In Microsoft PowerPoint, templates allow you to apply pre-designed styles and graphics (see Figure 4.1).

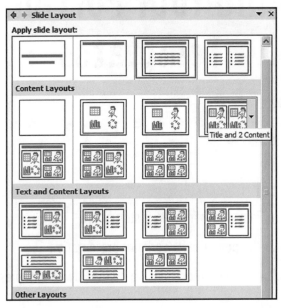

4.1 Select an appropriate slide layout format for each screen of your portfolio before you enter the text from your storyboard.

Step by Step

Before you begin, make sure you have completed your storyboard, as directed in the previous chapter.

1. Start Microsoft PowerPoint. Go to File > New. Select the Blank Presentation. This is the default style of plain black type on a white background.

2. Go to File > Save. In the Save As dialog box, navigate to the Portfolio Files folder you created in Chapter 2. In the Portfolio Files folder, save this new file as Portfolio.ppt. This is the first file you will place within this folder that is outside of the subfolders, as shown in Figure 4.2.

4.2 Save the Portfolio.ppt file into the Portfolio Files folder.

3. Go to Format > Slide Layout. This displays the Slide Layout pane along the right side of your screen. You will use this pane to choose your templates. To see the slide name, point to the slide. A ScreenTip will display with the name of the slide.

4. For the first slide, select Title Slide from the Slide Layout, if it is not already selected. Click in the top text box and type your portfolio title (this should match the title on your storyboard). In the text box below the title, type your name and contact information. Alternatively, you can copy and paste this information from your resume.

. . . .

Copying Text from Your Resume Document

If you want to copy and paste text from your resume, then use the plain-text version you created (this way, you won't have to remove or adjust formatting from the Microsoft Word document). Simply copy and paste the plain text to your PowerPoint slides and then adjust the formatting to match the content of the information.

. . . .

5. Go to Insert > New Slide to create a new slide. (You can also create a new slide by clicking the New Slide button on the Formatting toolbar.) From the Slide Layout pane, select the bulleted list layout, called Title and Text. In the title text box, type **Table of Contents**. Using your storyboard as a reference, type each of the categories in the text box—the categories will be formatted as a bulleted list automatically.

6. For each storyboard panel, create a new slide and add the storyboard text. For each of the slides, select the slide layout that most closely matches the look of the slides from the storyboard you created. See Figures 4.3 and 4.4.

Experience

- Current Job Title, Date – present
- Company Name, Address
- Accomplishment or special responsibility 1
- Accomplishment or special responsibility 2
- Accomplishment or special responsibility 3

4.3 Slide with text copied and pasted from the plain-text version of the resume.

Experience

Current Job Title, Date – present
Company Name, Address
- Accomplishment or special responsibility 1
- Accomplishment or special responsibility 2
- Accomplishment or special responsibility 3

4.4 Slide with bullets removed from lines 1 and 2 (the non-list items) and job title made bold.

7. After the complete contents of your resume are placed on slides, create a single blank slide as the last slide. You will need this blank slide later to construct links to your samples. Your presentation should now look similar to Figure 4.5.

8. Save your work.

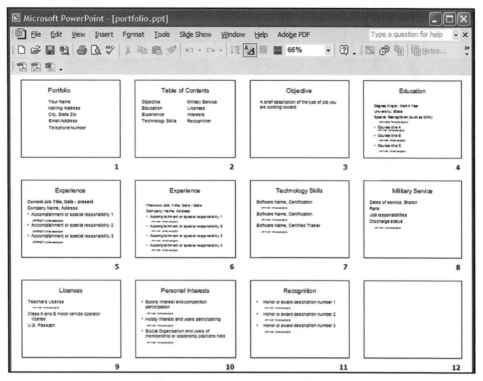

4.5 These are the 11 slides created using the demonstration resume and storyboard. Don't forget to add a blank slide at the end.

Select Your Portfolio Design

Slide presentation programs, such as Microsoft PowerPoint, offer templates and themes that can be applied at any time to a single slide or to the entire presentation. These pre-designed themes usually include a set of colors and graphics for the background and text, as well as bullets and other graphical elements that are part of the theme design. Themes are an easy way to achieve a professional design look. This is one of the things that makes this software an easy tool to use for designing a digital portfolio. The trick is to find and select a well-designed theme appropriate for a professional portfolio. A theme is just one way to bring professionalism and consistency to your design.

What is consistency? In design, *consistency* is a common color theme or graphic treatment throughout a document. Consistency is an easy way to make your portfolio as easy to review as possible. For example, if the same navigational item, such as a Home button, is in the same place on every page, the person reviewing your portfolio doesn't have to take his or her mind off of your work to figure out what the buttons on each page do. That is one of the primary goals in the design of this portfolio—make it as easy as possible for people to open it, move through it, and view your work.

Choosing a Design Template for Your PowerPoint File

Now that you have created your PowerPoint file, it's time to give your portfolio style. There are three ways in which you can add style:

- Use the PowerPoint Design Templates that are already loaded in the Design Templates palette on your desktop. Microsoft offers some beautiful, contemporary templates perfectly suited to a broad range of career portfolios (see Figure 4.6).

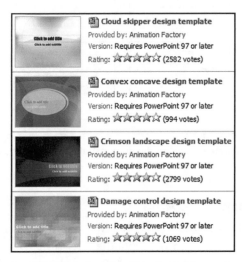

4.6 Examples of the free PowerPoint design templates from Microsoft.com: http://office.microsoft.com/en-us/templates/.

- Create your own templates. Of course, if you are skilled in the graphic arts, you can create your own background and color themes for a customized or more personal look.

- Download and use templates from the Web. Additional templates are freely available through the Microsoft Web site and other sites. Figure 4.7 shows examples of free PowerPoint templates that are appropriate for portfolios. The Microsoft site contains step-by-step instructions for downloading and installing templates on your computer.

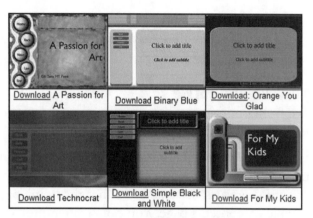

4.7 Look for free PowerPoint templates with navigation buttons at Brainy Betty: http://www.brainybetty.com/preprogrammedpowerpointtemplates.htm.

Finding Templates to Use with a Mac

If you are looking for PowerPoint templates for the Mac, go to the Microsoft Mactopia Web site: http://www.microsoft.com/mac/ and click on PowerPoint and Templates.

The design strategy used in this book takes advantage of the pre-designed templates available for Microsoft PowerPoint. Our instructions and strategy will describe the procedures for using templates. There are three things to consider before selecting your final template design:

- **Audience.** To choose an effective design for your portfolio, think about who the audience for your portfolio is. If it is for a job interview, then the type of company and the nature of its business might help you to make choices about your portfolio design. A banker, for instance, might want a solid and serious looking portfolio, whereas an architect probably wants a more creative look.

- **Legibility.** Pick a design that enhances your text and portfolio items. The person reviewing your portfolio should be able to easily read your text on the screen. If the design makes your text difficult to read, or if your text or examples clash with it, then choose another design template.

- **Navigation style.** *Navigation* is the method the viewer uses to move through your portfolio. When the portfolio is complete, it will be a file that is viewed primarily on a computer monitor. It is important to think about which way you want viewers to get around in your portfolio because it may make a difference in the design that you choose. (You will create these navigation buttons later in this chapter.)

Choosing a Navigation Style

People move from one page to another in a screen presentation, such as those created with PowerPoint, in three common ways:

- **Using buttons on the page, designed in PowerPoint.** A common navigational design is to use three buttons on each screen to let you go forward, back, and to either the home page (start page) or the table of contents page. You can create buttons in PowerPoint by using the button graphics or by using the Drawing tools to make shapes or letters to use as buttons (see Figures 4.8 and 4.9).

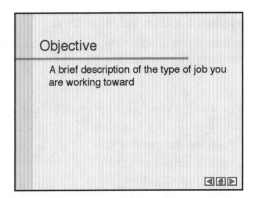

4.8 Using button graphics to create navigational buttons.

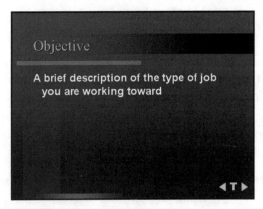

4.9 Using Drawing tools to create navigational buttons.

- **Using the Acrobat software interface.** Adobe Acrobat provides a way to navigate by using the forward and back keys on the computer keyboard or by clicking anywhere inside the presentation screen. To use this method, your final portfolio would have to be set up so that the Acrobat navigation shows—not as a full screen presentation. If you choose this method of navigation, you do not need to have or add graphic buttons in your design template. See Figures 4.10 and 4.11.

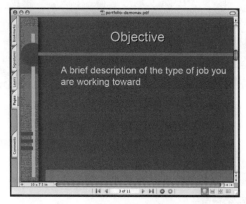

4.10 You can use Acrobat's built-in navigation to move around the presentation.

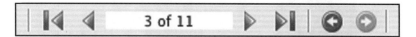

4.11 A close-up of Acrobat's built-in navigation.

- **Using a menu placed on each page of the presentation, designed in PowerPoint.** This is a Web-like navigation design, using words that are linked in Acrobat to allow users to go from almost any screen in the portfolio to any other. In a portfolio, you would probably allow users to jump to sections rather than making every page of the portfolio available in the on-page navigation. PowerPoint templates are available with navigation buttons, as shown in Figure 4.12, or you can just add text to any design to turn an area of the screen into a navigation bar, as shown in Figure 4.13.

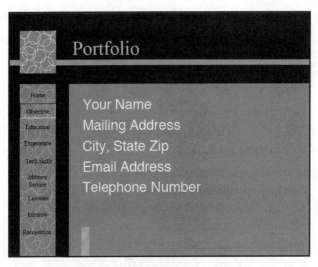

4.12 Using text links to navigate.

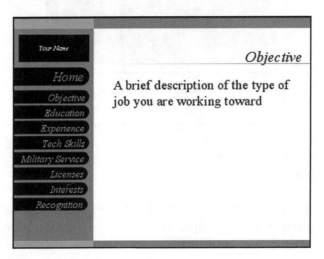

4.13 Using graphic buttons to navigate.

Now, use Worksheet 4.1 to decide on a navigation style for your presentation.

4.1 Deciding On a Navigation Style

Directions: Take a moment to reflect on the following questions and then write an answer to each.

1. What are the advantages of each of the preceding navigation styles?

   _____

   _____

2. What are the disadvantages of each of the preceding navigation styles?

   _____

   _____

3. Which navigation style most closely matches your design template? Is this the style you are using for your presentation?

   _____

   _____

When you have chosen a design template that matches your navigation style, you are ready to proceed to the next step: applying your design template.

Applying a Design Template for Your PowerPoint File

The hard part is choosing the design template that's right for your portfolio. The easy part is applying that template.

Step by Step

1. In PowerPoint, in the Slide Layout pane, locate and then click the downward-pointing triangle. From the menu that displays, click Slide Design – Design Templates. (Alternatively, go to Format > Slide Design.) In the Slide Design pane that displays on the right side of your screen, click Design Templates.

2. Select a template by clicking on it, as shown in Figure 4.14. The theme will be immediately reflected in your slide.

4.14 The Design Templates palette with available styles.

3. Apply your selection to all of your slides. In Slide Sorter view, check to make sure all of your portfolio slides have the template applied, as shown in Figure 4.15.

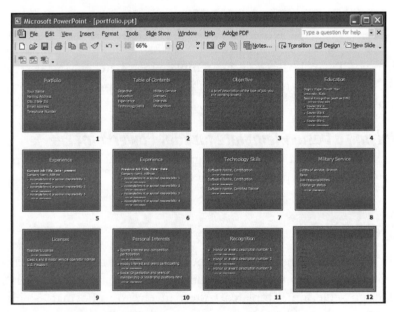

4.15 Slide Sorter view of portfolio with the design template applied.

4. Save your work.

Putting Master Slides to Use

If you have used PowerPoint before, you have probably worked with master slides. *Master slides* contain the information and formatting of a template that goes on every slide. Some design templates are comprised of a single master slide, whereas other templates have a set of master slides with alternative designs for different parts of the presentation. For example, a master slide set might include a Title Master and a Slide Master, each with a different but coordinated graphic treatment. For this project, you will create an additional master slide.

Creating a Blank Master Slide

When you created your design template, you included a blank slide at the end. By default this slide uses the same styles as the Slide Master. Because you want a different navigation on the blank slide than on the rest of the slides in the portfolio (you no longer need to go forward), you need to make a new Slide Master for the blank slide.

Step by Step

1. If necessary, start PowerPoint and open your portfolio file.

2. Go to View > Master > Slide Master to open the master slides.

3. If you have only one master, then duplicate that slide. If you have two masters, then duplicate the one that is not the Title Master. To duplicate the master, select the thumbnail in the Slide pane, right-click, and choose Copy.

Understanding Which Slides Are Which

When in the Slide Master view, you can identify the thumbnails of the masters by reading the ScreenTip when holding your mouse over the thumbnail. You can also identify the masters by looking at the status bar at the bottom of the window.

4. Right-click in the Slide pane and choose Paste.

5. If you had two masters and they were linked, both of them will copy. Just select the new Title Master and delete it so that you have three masters: one Title Master and two Slide Masters.

6. In the new Slide Master, delete the Object Area text box in the center of the slide but leave the Title Area text box at the top of the slide, as shown in Figure 4.16. You can also delete the small text boxes along the bottom of the master slide by clicking each box and then pressing Delete because you won't be using them in this portfolio design.

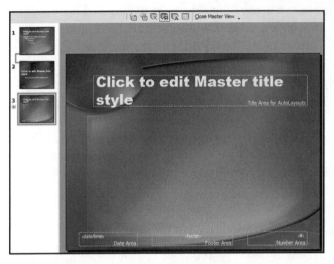

4.16 The view of the master slides with a new master added.

7. In the Slide pane, right-click on the new Slide Master thumbnail and select Rename Master.

8. Type the new name for this master: **Blank Master**.

9. Click on Close Master View to return to your presentation.

10. Click on your Blank slide in the Pages pane.

11. If the Slide Design pane is not open on your desktop, go to Format > Slide Design to open it.

12. You will find your new master in the Design Templates menu under Used in this Presentation with the original slide master. With your blank slide selected in the Pages pane, right-click on the Blank Master thumbnail in the Design Templates pane and choose Apply To Selected Slides (see Figure 4.17).

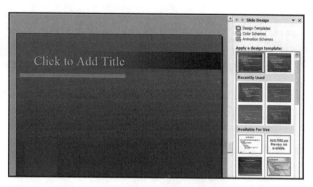

4.17 The view of the presentation with the blank slide selected and the Design Templates pane open.

With your master slides now in place, you can begin adding navigational elements.

Adding Navigation to Each Slide

If the design template you chose included navigation, you can skip this section. However, if navigation is not part of the design template, you will have to add the graphics or text to each slide.

Each slide master will get a different set of navigation graphics. The title master slide needs only a forward button. The slide master used for the body of the portfolio needs forward, back, and home buttons. The Blank Master needs only a back button.

These could be buttons from the Action Buttons palette or your own creation of shapes or letters using the Drawing tools to represent navigation. It isn't important to have the navigation functioning at this point. The graphics or navigation text will simply be placed on your master slide so it appears in a consistent location on each screen of your PowerPoint portfolio file.

The following sections provide step-by-step directions for the different ways that you can create buttons for navigation:

- By using the Action Buttons menu to create buttons automatically

- By creating graphic buttons using the Drawing tools

- By creating a text navigation menu

After examining these methods, you can decide which you are going to use for your portfolio. The following worksheet will help you decide which method is right for you.

4.2 Deciding Between Buttons and Text Menus for Navigation

Directions: Take a moment to reflect on the following questions and then write an answer to each.

1. What are the advantages of using buttons? Of a text menu?

_____

_____

2. What are the disadvantages of using buttons? Of a text menu?

_____

_____

3. Which method will you use to add navigation to your presentation? Why?

_____

_____

After you have chosen between button navigation and text menu, you are ready to proceed to the next step: creating the buttons and text menu. The following sections show you how.

Using the Action Buttons Menu to Create Buttons

PowerPoint allows you to create buttons automatically by using the Action Buttons menu. Placing navigation on each master automatically places that button on each slide that the master controls.

For now, these buttons are just graphics, not working PowerPoint links. Instead, you will use Acrobat to do the actual linking. You will need to create both forward and back buttons.

Step by Step

To begin, you will create a Forward button on the Title Master:

1. If necessary, start PowerPoint and open your portfolio file.

2. Go to View > Master > Slide Master. You will find that you have three slide masters: Title, Slide, and Blank. On the Title Master, you will create a Forward button.

3. Go to Slide Show > Action Buttons and then click the graphic symbol for Forward or Next (see Figure 4.18). Because this is the first slide of the presentation, this is the only button you need.

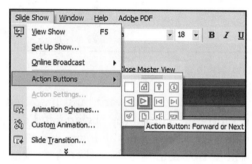

4.18 Selecting the Forward action button.

4. Notice that the cursor changes to a crosshair. Click and drag a rectangle in the lower-right corner of the screen. When you release the mouse, the forward (right-pointing) button will appear.

5. From the menu that pops up, choose None. Later on, you will use Acrobat to turn this button into a working link. For now, you are using the Action Button tool to simply create the button graphic.

6. Double-click the button to open the Format AutoShape dialog box. In the dialog box, click the Color and Lines tab, if necessary, and select a Fill Color for the button (see Figure 4.19). The color should complement the design theme yet stand out enough so that viewers can easily find it. Click Preview to make sure you like your choice. When you are satisfied with the color, click OK.

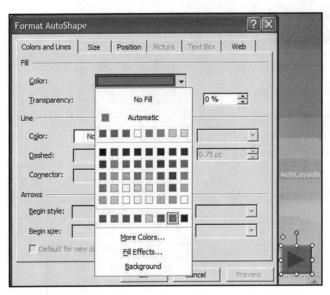

4.19 Setting the color and design of the button.

7. On the Title master, size the Forward button so that it is not too large. Next, position the button (by clicking and dragging it) to overlap the Number Area text box at the lower-right corner of the screen. You will not be using the Number Area text box in this portfolio design.

8. Double-click the Forward button, and in the Format AutoShape dialog box, click the Size tab. On a piece of scratch paper, note the values for Width and Height. Also, click the Position tab and write down the value for Vertical. You will need to know these measurements in order to size and align the Back button. Click OK.

9. Right-click on the completed Forward button and select Copy. You will paste a copy of the Forward button on the Slide Master so that you do not have to create a new Forward button for the Title Master.

10. Click on the Slide Master thumbnail in the Slide pane to bring the slide master into the workspace. Right-click on the Slide Master background and click Paste. The Forward button should appear on the Slide Master in the same position as it was on the Title Master.

Now you will create the Back button on the Slide Master:

11. Repeat steps 3–7, which you used to create the Forward button, to create the Back button. Be sure to select the backward button symbol in Step 3.

12. To size the Back button to be exactly the same size as the Forward button, double-click on the Back button and in the Format AutoShape dialog box, click the Size tab. Replace the Height and Width values with the values that you wrote down in Step 8 for the Forward button. Also, click the Position tab, and enter the Vertical value that you noted. Click OK.

13. To move the Back button closer to or farther from the Forward button, select the button and use the arrow keys on your keyboard. Don't move the buttons too closely together just yet—you still need to add a Home or Table of Contents button between them.

Now you will create the Home (or Table of Contents) button on the Slide Master:

14. Using the same method you used to create the first two buttons, create a Home button by selecting the Home icon from the Action Buttons palette. Position the Home button between the Forward and Back buttons so that the spacing between each of the buttons is equal. Your buttons should now look similar to those shown in Figure 4.20.

4.20 The completed button set on the Slide Master.

Finally, you will create a Back button on the Blank Master:

15. On the Title Master, which contains the three newly created buttons, click to select the Back button. Right-click and select Copy.

16. In the Slide pane, click on the new Blank Master thumbnail to bring that slide master into the workspace.

17. On the Blank Master background, right-click and select Paste. The Back button should appear on the Blank Master in the same position as it was on the Slide Master.

18. Close the Master View.

19. Check the placement of your buttons by going to the Slide Sorter view of your PowerPoint portfolio file. You should see the navigation buttons you just created on the slide masters on each slide of your portfolio.

20. When all buttons are complete, save your work.

Use the Drawing Tools for Better Looking Buttons

Although PowerPoint gives you the ability to change the color of the navigation buttons, you can't change the design very much. If you prefer to design your own graphics to use as buttons, you can use the Drawing tools in PowerPoint.

As with creating buttons by using the Action Buttons menu, the idea is to place the buttons on the master slides so that they appear automatically on each slide of the portfolio. Repeat the preceding steps for using the Action Buttons menu, but use the following steps when you're ready to create your buttons:

1. Go to the Drawing toolbar and select AutoShapes > Basic Shapes > Isosceles Triangle.

2. In the bottom-right corner of the master slide, click and drag the triangle shape. Do not deselect.

3. On the Drawing toolbar, choose Draw > Rotate or Flip > Rotate Right. This rotates the triangle so that it points to the right (or left).

4. On the Drawing toolbar, use the Fill Color, Line Color, and Line Style buttons to style your button.

To create the Home or Table of Contents button graphic, click the Text Box button on the Drawing toolbar. Then, on the slide, click between the Forward and Back buttons to insert the text box. Type the letter **H** (for Home) or **T** (for Table of Contents).

Creating a Text Navigation Menu

Text navigation is the easiest navigation of all to create. If this is your choice, be sure you have selected a Design Template that has an area that can contain the text navigation menu. In this example, the navigation will be placed in a panel of the design (see Figure 4.21). You can also find designs that have other graphic treatments that allow your text menu to be set apart and easy to read. You don't want to put a text menu on a busy pattern.

4.21 Example of text navigation.

Step by Step

1. If necessary, start PowerPoint and open your portfolio file.

2. Go to the Slide Master. Just like the other navigation styles, the text menu will be placed on the slide masters.

3. On the Drawing toolbar, click the Text Box button. In the area on the slide where you want the navigation to appear, position the crosshairs, click, and drag to create a box.

4. Type the word **Home** and press Enter.

5. Repeat Step 4 for each category title in your portfolio, substituting each category name for the word *Home*. This creates your navigation list.

6. Format the text so that it complements the style of the design template and theme you choose.

7. Copy and paste this navigation text box onto each of the remaining two master slides.

8. Close the Slide Master.

9. Check your navigation by going to the Slide Sorter view of your PowerPoint portfolio file. You should see the navigation you just created on the slide masters on each slide of your portfolio.

10. When all of the buttons are complete, save your work.

With the button graphics or navigation menu text in place for your presentation, you can begin preparing the links to your samples.

Adding Links to Examples of Your Work

The final step in creating your portfolio templates is to insert a line of placeholder text every time you have a portfolio item, such as a photograph or certificate of recognition, that you want to show. Later, you will change these lines of placeholder text into links to the items.

Each item that you want to link to needs a separate link (a single link cannot open multiple items). If you find that you have more than one item for a particular category, you can create a list. In the list, each word could be a link or you could make a link to another portfolio page where you could include multiple links to your artifacts. Although you can refer to the storyboard you created in the previous chapter for reference, this is where you should think carefully about how you want to attach your artifacts to your text descriptions.

Figure 4.22 shows an example of a line of placeholder text that will be used as a link. Notice that the artifact type is smaller than the portfolio information text—this is so that it doesn't compete with the primary information or make an overly busy page.

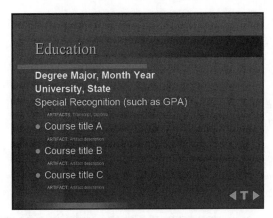

4.22 Placeholder text describes items for which links will later be created.

To indicate that the text will be a link, the link text should be shown in a different color. The most common design for a link is blue text with an underline—which is the most common and default format for links used on Web pages. If you are going to use this as your link style, you will want to avoid using a light blue background color for your slide. Otherwise, your text will not have enough contrast against the background color to be clearly visible.

Step by Step

1. If necessary, start PowerPoint and open your portfolio file.

2. For each item you want to link to, insert a line of text similar to that shown in Figure 4.22. Refer to your storyboard as necessary.

3. Save this PowerPoint file into the folder that also contains your folder of portfolio items. This is your *portfolio master file*. To make changes to the text or graphics in your portfolio later, you will need to come back to this file.

At this point your portfolio project folder should contain the portfolio PowerPoint document that you created in this chapter and a folder with your collected portfolio items, each numbered, named, and listed in your portfolio items list.

In This Chapter

Congratulations! You accomplished a lot in this chapter. The primary goal was to create your portfolio template, which you began by choosing a design template. Next, you chose a navigation style for your portfolio and began setting up your slide masters. On your slide masters, you created navigational buttons that viewers could use to move around within your presentation. Finally, you created placeholder text so that you could add links from your presentation to the portfolio items you want to show. In the next chapter, you will prepare the digital versions of your portfolio items.

4.3 Idea Starters

Directions: Take a moment to reflect on the following questions and then write an answer to each.

1. Were you able to fit your content comfortably and consistently on each page of your portfolio? If not, what did you do?

_____

_____

(continued)

(continued)

4.3 Idea Starters

2. How does the design template you chose relate to your audience or the type of career you want?

_____

_____

3. Which style of navigation did you choose? Why?

_____

_____

4. Do you have other ideas for adding navigational elements to your presentation?

_____

_____

5. Can you think of other presentations in which you could apply the skills you learned in this chapter?

_____

_____

Size and Optimize
Your Artifacts

In This Chapter

- Explore the most common formats for saving your electronic files
- Convert your non-digital items to electronic format
- Save your digital files in common formats
- Create PDFs
- Size your digital files for easy viewing

After you collect and organize all of your portfolio items, you need a way to prepare each of them for easy viewing within your digital portfolio. In this chapter, we will give you several options for converting or resaving your various portfolio items into formats that are easily viewable by others.

Attaching Samples of Your Work to Your Portfolio

There are two ways to include an item in your PDF portfolio:

- Link an electronic copy of the artifact so that when the artifact is clicked in the PDF, the artifact opens in the program in which it was created.

- Convert an electronic copy of the artifact into a PDF or insert (embed) a copy of the artifact in a PDF page.

Although you can link an artifact so that the program that created it launches and the document opens up in it, this is not the best method for presenting your portfolio because it requires that the viewer have all of the same software—and, in some cases, the same version of the software—that you have on your computer in order to see your files. In the event the viewer does not have a piece of software when he or she clicks on your artifact link, he or she will receive an error message instead of seeing your artifact.

The more reliable way to add artifacts to your portfolio is to convert them into PDFs or embed them in a PDF page. This method is preferred because it does not require that the person viewing your portfolio have any special software to view examples of your work.

In this book, we will use the second method of adding artifacts whenever possible. However, we will also use the linking method for some artifacts, but only in special circumstances because of the potential for problems.

Exploring the Common Electronic Formats

The first step in the process of adding artifacts to your PDF portfolio is to get a copy of each of your artifacts into an electronic format. With electronic copies of your work, you will be able to link to your artifact or embed it within a PDF. The goal in this chapter is to get as many of your artifacts as possible into one of the four common file formats shown in Table 5.1.

Table 5.1 Recommended File Formats		
EXTENSION	**DESCRIPTION**	**ADVANTAGES**
PDF	Portable Document Format	Can be created in many programs through Save As or by printing to PDF through the Print dialog box if Adobe Acrobat is installed on the computer.
JPEG	Common format for photographs and graphics	Can be created in many programs through Save As or by Export. Commonly created using paint programs, Adobe Photoshop or Elements.
AVI	Common motion media or video format played by a Windows media player or plug-in	AVI files can be produced on some cameras, but more often they are exported after editing in video software such Premiere or Pinnacle. AVI files contain an audio and a video track.
SWF	Common animation format	Can be created in several Macromedia programs, including Flash, as well as Adobe Illustrator.

Getting Your Samples into a Common Electronic Format

You have several options for converting your artifacts to one of these four electronic formats. Of course, if you have a paper or other non-electronic format, you will have to first get that item into an electronic format. If you created the artifact using software, check to see whether that software will allow you to Save As or Export the file to one of these formats. If not, you may need an additional program or procedure to make the conversion.

Table 5.2 contains a list of various document types and the programs that will convert them.

Table 5.2 Suggestions for Converting Various Portfolio Items	
TO CONVERT THIS...	**USE THIS...**
To convert Microsoft Office documents, photographs, Web pages, and images to PDF files	Adobe Acrobat Professional 7.0
To convert digital video to AVI	Video-editing software such as Pinnacle Studio (Windows), Adobe Premiere, and Apple QuickTime Pro.
To convert analog video to digital video	A digital video camera or deck and an analog deck, cables, and a computer with digital video editing software such as Pinnacle, iMovie (Mac), or Premiere.
To convert digital audio to AVI	Audio editing software or video editing software like Premiere, Pinnacle, and Apple QuickTime Pro.
To convert analog audio to digital audio	An audio tape player, cable, audio input (on computer or external device), and audio editing software (see digital audio above).
To convert Flash animation and animated GIFs	Acrobat Professional, which converts Flash files within the program. For animated GIFs, open them in a video editing program such as Adobe Premiere and then export as an AVI.
To create PDFs from any non-motion document	Use the computer to create an image of a non-moving document that is displayed on the screen and then save it in Photoshop as a PDF.

Converting a document from its original format to one of the four formats you will use to build the portfolio can be as easy as re-opening the document in the program that created it and then resaving it in one of the four commonly accepted formats. For some documents, however, the process will be to export the file to a new format.

Table 5.3 provides an overview of the different methods you can use to convert your documents. After you determine which of the methods you might need to use for your artifacts, the sections that follow this worksheet describe the specific procedures you will need.

Table 5.3 How to Convert Your Portfolio Items

IF YOU HAVE THIS TYPE OF ITEM...	YOU CAN USE THIS SOFTWARE...	...TO CONVERT YOUR SAMPLE TO THESE FORMATS	
Word processing document	Microsoft Word, Open Office, Star Office, AppleWorks, Apple Pages	Paper printout	See the section *"From Paper to PDF"* later in this chapter.
		.doc file	See *"From Word Document to PDF."*
PDF document	Adobe Acrobat and Acrobat Elements	Paper printout	See *"From Paper to PDF."*
		PDF file	No conversion needed if you want to attach it with a hyperlink to the portfolio. If you want an image of the PDF page to place on your PowerPoint template, Save As JPEG using Adobe Acrobat Professional.
Slide presentation	Microsoft PowerPoint, Apple Keynote	Paper printout	See *"From Paper to PDF."*
		Native (such as PPT, KEY)	See *"From PowerPoint to PDF."*
Photograph	Adobe Photoshop and Photoshop Elements, Microsoft Paint, Google Picassa, Apple iPhoto, Ulead PhotoImpact	Print	See *"From Paper to PDF."*
		Native PSD or other digital file	In the native PSD file, go to Save As and select Photoshop PDF if you want to attach it to the portfolio through a hyperlink. If you want to place the image on a template screen, Save As a JPEG.

IF YOU HAVE THIS TYPE OF ITEM...	YOU CAN USE THIS SOFTWARE...	...TO CONVERT YOUR SAMPLE TO THESE FORMATS	
Graphic image	Adobe Illustrator and Photoshop, Jasc Paint Shop, Microsoft Paint	Paper printout	See *"From Paper to PDF."*
		Native AI digital file	If you want to attach the image to the portfolio through a hyperlink, in the native AI file, go to Save As and select Adobe PDF. If you want to place the image on a template screen, choose Save For Web.
Web page	Macromedia Dreamweaver, Microsoft FrontPage, Mozilla Composer	Web site	See *"Create PDF from Web Page."*
Video	Apple Final Cut, QuickTime Pro, and iMovie; Adobe Premiere; Pinnacle Studio; Microsoft Windows Movie Maker	Analog tape (such as VHS)	Using a digital video camera and VHS player, convert the analog data to digital data. There are also special decks that do this conversion. The goal is to end up with a digital video format that can be edited and saved as an AVI file to embed in a screen of your PDF portfolio.
		Digital tape (such as miniDV)	Using your digital video camera, transfer the file to your desktop and edit in a video-editing program. Then save as an AVI file to embed in a screen of your PDF portfolio.

(continued)

(continued)

Table 5.3 How to Convert Your Portfolio Items

IF YOU HAVE THIS TYPE OF ITEM...	YOU CAN USE THIS SOFTWARE...	...TO CONVERT YOUR SAMPLE TO THESE FORMATS	
Audio	Peak Studio Bias, Apple Logic, Sound Forge, Acid, Adobe Audition, Apple QuickTime Pro	Analog tape (such as Type I)	With the right computer setup, you can stream analog audio to your desktop to edit. If you don't have the right setup, an external device can be purchased to go between your analog tape deck and your computer. Audio editing software can save the file as an AVI file.
		Digital tape (such as DAT)	Using audio editing software, or even video editing software that allows separate editing of the audio track, save as an AVI file with audio track only (no video track).
Animation	Adobe ImageReady, Premiere, and Final Cut Pro; Macromedia Flash; Newtek Light Wave	Digital animation file (such as SWF, GIF)	If you have an SWF Flash format animation, you can place it on an Adobe Acrobat portfolio page. If you have an animated GIF file, you need to convert it to an AVI file to place it on a PDF page. Use a video-editing program such as Premiere to open and export the GIF as an AVI file.
Multimedia presentation	Macromedia Director and Flash, Apple QuickTime Pro	Digital file (such as EXE, DCR, MOV, SWF)	If the presentation is saved as a SWF or AVI file, it can be placed in a PDF page. Director executable files (.exe) will lose their interactive properties if saved as an AVI, so save them as Shockwave files to play as a link to the external document.

IF YOU HAVE THIS TYPE OF ITEM…	YOU CAN USE THIS SOFTWARE…	…TO CONVERT YOUR SAMPLE TO THESE FORMATS	
Page layouts	QuarkXPress, Adobe InDesign, Apple Pages, Microsoft Publisher	Paper printout	See *"From Paper to PDF."*
		Native (such as IND, QXP)	Choose Save As or Print to PDF to hyperlink the document to the PDF portfolio. Make screen prints of the pages to place images on PowerPoint template screens.
Database	Microsoft Access and Excel, Filemaker Pro	Paper printout	See *"From Paper to PDF."*
		Native (such as XLS or MDB)	If you want to hyperlink the database file to the portfolio, then the viewer has to have the software to run the file. Another option is to save the database file as HTML and then use Acrobat to create a PDF that can link to the portfolio. Make screen prints of the pages to place images on PowerPoint template screens.
Diagram	Visio, Inspiration	Paper printout	See *"From Paper to PDF."*
		Native (such as INS)	Save the file as a JPEG to place an image of the chart on a Power-Point slide.
CAD	IntelliCAD, AutoCAD	Paper printout	See *"From Paper to PDF."*
		Native	Choose Save As PDF to attach the file to a hyperlink made in the PDF portfolio. Make screen prints of the pages to place images of the CAD screens on PowerPoint template slides.

(continued)

(continued)

Table 5.3 How to Convert Your Portfolio Items			
IF YOU HAVE THIS TYPE OF ITEM...	**YOU CAN USE THIS SOFTWARE...**	**...TO CONVERT YOUR SAMPLE TO THESE FORMATS**	
Statistics	SPSS, Systat	Paper printout	See *"From Paper to PDF."*
		Native	Save the reports as HTML and create PDF pages using Adobe Acrobat. Make screen prints of the pages to place images of the Statistics screens on PowerPoint template slides.
Music notation	Sibelius, MusicTek SmartScore	Paper printout	See *"From Paper to PDF."*
		Native	Save the notation as a TIFF file or make screen prints of the pages to place images of the notation screens on PowerPoint template slides. Save the native file as a PDF to attach to a hyperlink on the PDF portfolio page.
		Audio file	If you produce an audio file from the notation, save it as an AVI file format or place on a PDF portfolio page.

Using Acrobat to Create PDFs

Adobe Acrobat Professional gives you several ways to format documents as PDF files. The following sections include instructions for using Acrobat to create PDFs from four types of documents:

- Paper
- Word documents
- PowerPoint presentations
- Web pages

Keeping Your Files Organized

As you create or convert files for each of your portfolios, be sure to save them in the Portfolio Files folder you created in Chapter 2. If your file is already in electronic format, be sure to maintain the number and name of the file that you assigned to it in Worksheet 2.2, "Creating a List of Portfolio Items," in Chapter 2.

From Paper to PDF

When converting paper artifacts to PDF, you have two options:

- Scan your document and save it as a PDF file.

- Use Acrobat to create the PDF directly from your scanner.

Which option you choose depends on the capabilities of your hardware and software.

Saving a Scan in PDF Format

To scan and save document in PDF format:

Note

For specific instructions on using your scanner, see the scanner documentation that came with your scanner.

1. Place the document on the flatbed of your scanner.

2. Start your scanning software. You should find settings to control the scanning process in your software.

3. Select to scale the document at 100%. Choose a resolution of 72 to 96 pixels per inch, which is the resolution of most monitors. The *resolution* is fineness of detail of your computer screen.

   If you choose a larger number, the document may become so big on the computer screen that it is difficult to view or read. The recommended settings should make the document on the screen the same size as the paper document.

Understanding Resolution

To display your document on a computer screen, you will want to use a resolution of 72 to 96 pixels per inch. In contrast, images to be output to paper would be formatted at a resolution expressed in dots per inch, which is a measurement related to the printing screens at which the images would be produced.

4. Scan the document.

5. If your software allows you to save your scan in PDF format, save the document as a PDF. If your software cannot save directly to PDF, skip to Step 6.

6. If your scanning software does not offer PDF as a format for saving the scanned file, you will need to first save the scan as a JPEG and then convert the JPEG to a PDF, as described in the remaining steps. See the section "Sizing Your Artifacts" later in the chapter for details on sizing and saving JPEG images.

7. Start Adobe Acrobat Professional.

8. Go to File > Create PDF > From File and navigate to the JPEG file you just created.

9. Select the JPEG and click OK. Acrobat will convert the JPEG to a PDF that you will see in the window on the screen.

10. Go to File > Save and save the file in the PDF format into your PDF folder with the number and name you had used to identify the file in Worksheet 2.2, "Creating a List of Portfolio Items," in Chapter 2.

Scanning from Acrobat

To scan a document in Acrobat:

1. Place the document on the flatbed of your scanner.

2. Start Adobe Acrobat Professional.

3. Go to File > Create PDF > From Scanner. A window will pop up with selections for the scan.

What to Do If Your Scanner Reads "None"

If the pull-down menu next to Scanner says None, you will need to install either a TWAIN or Capture plug-in to make this option work. See your scanner documentation and Adobe Acrobat help for instructions for your particular scanner and computer operating system.

4. Click Scan and then Save the resulting PDF file. Be sure to save the new PDF file into your PDF folder with the number and name you had used to identify the file in Worksheet 2.2, "Creating a List of Portfolio Items," in Chapter 2.

From Word Document to PDF

You have two options for converting Word documents into PDF format. If the Adobe Acrobat PDFMaker toolbar is available, you can click the Adobe PDF button. Otherwise, you need to convert the document by using the Print dialog box.

Using the Adobe PDF Button

To use PDFMaker:

1. Start Microsoft Word and open the document you want to convert to a PDF.

2. On the Adobe Acrobat PDFMaker toolbar, click on the Convert to Adobe PDF button, as shown in Figure 5.1. (If the toolbar does not display, click Views > Toolbars > Adobe Acrobat PDFMaker.)

5.1 Click the Adobe PDF button to easily convert Word documents to PDF format.

3. Navigate to your PDFs folder as the place where you want to save the new PDF and then click OK. A status bar will appear and display the progress of the conversion. When the conversion is complete, click Done.

Using the Print Dialog Box

To use File > Print:

1. Start Word and open the document you want to convert to a PDF.

2. Go to File > Print.

3. In the Print dialog box, choose PDF from the list of Printer choices, as shown in Figure 5.2. Click OK.

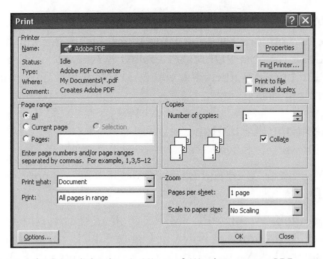

5.2 You can also use the Print dialog box in Microsoft Word to create a PDF.

4. Navigate to your PDFs folder as the place where you want to save the new PDF and click Save.

From PowerPoint to PDF

When it comes time to turn your PowerPoint presentation into a PDF, you have two options. You can create a PDF slide show (see Figure 5.3) or you can create single pages that display small images of the PowerPoint slides, similar to the PowerPoint handouts (see Figure 5.4). Both options make use of the Print dialog box in PowerPoint. Pick the way that suits your portfolio presentation or purpose best.

5.3 You can display your PowerPoint slides in Acrobat as a slide show—one at a time.

5.4 You can also display multiple PowerPoint slides in Acrobat on a single screen.

Printing to Slides

To print to slides:

1. Start PowerPoint and open the item you want to convert.

2. Go to File > Page Setup. In the Page Setup dialog box, under Orientation, under Slides, click to select the Landscape option button, as shown in Figure 5.5. (The landscape orientation means that the page will be wider than it is tall.)

5.5 The Page Setup dialog box allows you to set the print orientation to horizontal.

3. Go to File > Print. In the Print dialog box, use the Name drop-down menu to select Adobe PDF.

4. From the Print What drop-down menu, select Slides and click OK.

5. Navigate to your PDFs folder and click Save.

6. Go to File > Print and from the window select Adobe PDF from the pull-down list of printers and Slides from the Print What menu.

Printing to Handouts

To print to a handout:

1. Start PowerPoint and open the item you want to convert.

2. Go to File > Page Setup. In the Page Setup dialog box, under Orientation, under Notes, handouts & outline, click to select the Landscape option button.

3. Go to File > Print. In the Print dialog box, use the Name drop-down menu to select Adobe PDF (see Figure 5.6).

4. Select Handouts and the number of slides you want to see on each page from the Print What drop-down menu (see Figure 5.6).

5. Click on Print, navigate to your PDFs folder, and click Save. You may need to wait a few minutes while the PDF file is created.

6. Go to File > Print and select Adobe PDF from the Print menu and Handouts with the number of slides you want on each page from the Print What menu (as shown in Figure 5.6).

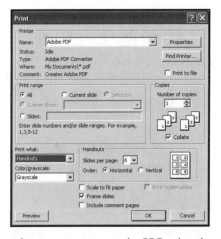

5.6 Use the Print What drop-down menu to create the PDF as handouts.

From Web Page to PDF

If you have created Web pages, whether they reside on your desktop, external storage device or on a Web server, you can convert them to PDFs for presentation within your portfolio. Although we do not show a Web page in the example, you may need this procedure for your own work.

Creating a PDF from within Acrobat

1. Start Adobe Acrobat Professional.

2. Go to File > Create PDF > From Web page (see Figure 5.7).

3. In the Create PDF from Web Page dialog box, click Browse to navigate to the Web page file (HTML file) and click OK. Or, if the Web page is on the Web, type the URL (Web address).

4. Click Create. When the Web page is converted to a PDF, save the new file to the PDFs folder of your Portfolio folder.

5.7 Select a Web page stored on your desktop to convert to a PDF.

- -

Creating an Image of Your Computer Screen

Anything your computer can display can be captured as a single image, called a *screen capture, screen snap,* or *screen print.* You can use your computer's built-in screen capture feature as an easy way to create images of your files.

1. Arrange your computer screen the way you want the file to look in the image.

2. Press the Print Screen key on your keyboard.

3. Start a paint program such as Microsoft Paint or Adobe Photoshop. Go to File > New and use the default dimensions.

4. Go to Edit > Paste. The screen image will appear in the new window.

5. Crop the image if necessary.

6. Go to File > Save and save as either a PDF file or a JPEG image.

- -

Sizing Your Artifacts

As you format your samples, there is something else to consider. That is, what size will the new file be? A general rule of thumb is that because the file will be viewed on a computer screen, it should be saved at the resolution of most computer screens—72 pixels per inch—and able to fit in the dimension of 800 pixels wide by 600 pixels tall.

Before you change the size of your image, you need to understand the difference between image size and resolution. The image size is the actual dimension—measured in pixels—of the image, whereas the resolution is the amount of space that the pixels are printed over. When you change the resolution, you change the printed size of the image. When you change the image size, you also change the number of pixels in the image, which can change the quality of the image. For the purposes of this book, you will want to set up your images so that the image contains approximately 72 pixels per inch and has an image size equal to or less than 800 pixels wide by 600 pixels tall.

Saving Images That Have Important Details

There are exceptions to preceding rule of thumb, of course. If you want to include an image that has small elements that are not easily seen in a reduced size or resolution, then you would save that file at a larger dimension or resolution. Although the viewer would have to scroll horizontally and vertically to see the entire document, he would be able to view the details.

Step by Step

1. Start Adobe Photoshop and open the image file. (You could also use a program such as Microsoft Paint, but the directions will vary.)

2. Go to Image > Size. In the Image Size dialog box, change either the image dimension or the resolution, as shown in Figure 5.8. Be sure to check Constrain Proportions so that the image is not distorted— that is, make sure the image size and resolution change together.

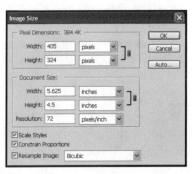

5.8 The Image Size dialog box of Adobe Photoshop showing the image dimensions (height and width) and resolution.

3. Go to File > Save As. In the Save As dialog box, chooose JPEG from the Format drop-down menu and click Save. In the JPEG Options dialog box, choose Medium for the quality. Click the Preview check box so that you can preview the quality and click OK.

4. If you are happy with the look and size of the JPEG file, go to File > Save. If not, repeat Steps 1–4 until you are satisfied with the results. You can choose High for an image with better quality—but at the cost of a larger file size.

Note

Always save your original file as well as the re-sized or formatted new files (File > Save As).

In This Chapter

In this chapter, you learned about the importance of attaching samples of your work to your portfolio. Additionally, you explored how to convert your digital and non-digital items into the most common and easily viewed electronic formats. You also paid special attention to how size your samples appropriately. In the next chapter, you will prepare special pages and create the portfolio PDF.

5.1 Idea Starters

Directions: Take a moment to reflect on the following questions and then write an answer to each.

1. What tips or tricks for converting files to common electronic formats can you share with others?

_____

_____

2. In what situations might it be useful to create and use a screen capture?

_____

_____

(continued)

(continued)

5.1 Idea Starters

3. Were you unhappy with the quality of any of the images you converted? If so, how were you able to fix the problem?

_____

_____

4. Do you have any samples that need to be shown at larger than 800 pixels by 600 pixels? If so, list them here.

_____

_____

5. Please describe what happens to an image when you change its size without also changing its resolution.

_____

_____

Prepare Special Pages and Create the Portfolio PDF

In This Chapter

- Insert sample images of your work into the PowerPoint presentation
- Create slides to hold your audio and video samples
- Convert your PowerPoint presentation into a PDF

With the conversion of your digital and non-digital files to one of the common file formats complete, the next step in the portfolio development process is to prepare special pages that can display those items. In the previous chapters, you've focused primarily on creating the textual content and placeholder links to samples of your work. Now, you will add your JPEG images to the end of your existing presentation, as well as create placeholder slides for your audio and video files. And finally, you will convert your presentation to PDF format.

Preparing Portfolio Pages to Display Samples of Your Work

In this section, you evaluate all of your links to your samples and then create the slides you will need. (You will not need to do anything for your samples that are documents.) You will add slides and insert any files you converted to the JPEG format into your PowerPoint presentation so that you can begin showing samples of your work. You will also prepare slides that will contain the audio and video files, although you won't insert the actual files into the PDF until the next chapter.

Listing Files to Include in Your Presentation

To begin, list each item you want to include in your portfolio so that you can create the PowerPoint slide it needs. (If you are linking to a document, you don't need to do anything.) If you are linking to a JPEG image, you can choose to link to the image or to create a special slide on which you can place the image. If you are linking to a video or audio sample, you need to prepare a placeholder for the file. The easiest way to do this is to print a copy of your PowerPoint presentation, evaluate each slide, and make a list of the links to each type of item.

You Can Skip This Section If...

If you do not have any small JPEG, video, or audio files to add to your portfolio, you can skip to the section "Creating the Portfolio PDF File" later in this chapter.

Step by Step

1. Locate the copy of the PowerPoint presentation you saved at the end of Chapter 4. Recall that this is your portfolio master file.

2. Go to File > Print. In the Print dialog box, choose Handouts from the Print What drop-down menu. Under Handouts, choose 3 from the Slides per page drop-down menu. Click OK to print the slides from your presentation.

3. For each slide, evaluate your content. Use a a pen or pencil to list the link for each sample item you want to show:

   - If you are linking to a .DOC file, you don't need to do anything.

   - If you are linking to a JPEG image, you can link the image or prepare a slide for the image. Make a note on the printout of the file-name of the image or a note to insert a new slide.

   - If you are adding audio or video samples, you will need to prepare a new slide. Make a note that you need to insert a new slide.

These notes will become a visual reference as you create the necessary links and slides for your samples. This way, if the phone rings, you'll be able to find where you were and what you did and didn't do because you were checking the slides in order. The following three sections describe how to insert your samples or prepare slides to hold the samples.

Inserting JPEGs into Your Presentation

You probably have already converted your paper artifacts to JPEGs. Now you are ready to insert them into your PowerPoint presentation, using the following steps.

Step by Step

1. If necessary, start PowerPoint, open your portfolio file, and go to the blank slide at the end of your presentation.

2. Go to Insert > Duplicate Slide. A new blank slide will appear in your document so that the end of your presentation contains two blank slides.

3. Apply the New Slide Master to the new blank slide (Format > Slide Design).

4. Format the slide by choosing Format > Slide Layout and choose the Title and Content format. This will insert a title box and a content box, as shown in Figure 6.1. You will use the content box to insert an image.

6.1 Blank slide with Picture Format selected.

5. Go to Insert > Picture > From File (or double-click the Insert Picture area), navigate to your Artifacts folder, and then select the JPEG that you want to place on the slide, in this case a diploma.

Getting a Look at the Details

If you create a JPEG and place it on a slide, PowerPoint limits its size. If you want the viewer to see details, create a link to a larger JPEG or PDF. If the image is really large, however, viewers will have to scroll to see it.

6. If necessary, size the image to fit on your slide. Double-click on the image to open the Format Picture dialog box and click the Size tab.

Check the Constrain box. Type in a new measurement. You will find that the horizontal and vertical measurements adjust simultaneously to keep the image in proportion. Click OK to resize the image and return to the PowerPoint workspace, as shown in Figure 6.2.

7. In the title box, type the title text for the slide.

8. Repeat the preceding steps for all of the JPEG images of your work samples that you want to insert.

Adding a Design Touch

If you want, you can add additional text or images to slides. This is your portfolio, and you should design it according to the information you have and in the way you want to show it.

9. Save your work.

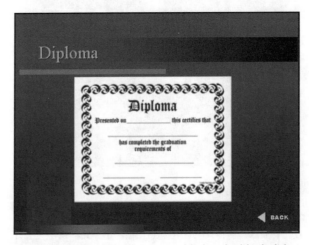

6.2 The heading "Diploma" and the diploma image added to the blank slide.

Preparing Slides So That You Can Add Video Files

Adding video samples to your portfolio is a great way to showcase your creative and technical talents. If any of the samples that you want to add to your portfolio are in video format, you need to prepare placeholder slides now so that you can place (or embed) the files in the PDF document so that they become part of the PDF. You will learn how to embed these files in the next chapter.

Step by Step

1. If necessary, start PowerPoint and open your portfolio file.

2. Go to the position where you want the video file to begin and choose Insert > Duplicate Slide to add new blank slide to your presentation. Apply the New Slide Master to the slide.

3. Format the new slide by choosing Format > Slide Layout and choose the Title Only slide. This will set up the slide so that it contains a title box and a blank area. You will use the blank area to insert your video file.

4. In the title box, type a title for your video slide. Figure 6.3 shows a slide prepared for a video file.

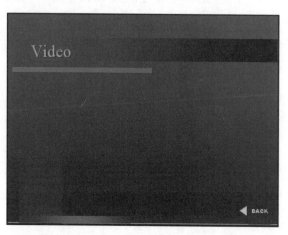

6.3 A placeholder slide prepared for a video file—the slide contains a title and a placeholder area for the video.

5. Repeat the preceding steps for all other video files you want to add.

6. Save your work.

After you have inserted all your JPEG images and after you have created all your placeholder slides for your audio and video files, you can finally create the PDF of your portfolio.

Preparing Slides So That You Can Embed Audio Files

If you have AVI artifacts that you want to play from a page of your portfolio, you have to prepare a slide now for the AVI to be embedded later in the PDF document. You will embed the AVI in an upcoming chapter.

Step by Step

1. Start PowerPoint and open your portfolio document.

2. Go to the Blank slide at the end of your PowerPoint portfolio file.

3. Select Insert > Duplicate Slide from the menu and a new blank slide will appear in your document.

4. Apply the New Slide Master to the slide.

5. Format the new slide by choosing Format > Slide Layout and Title Only from the menu of choices. This will give you a title panel and blank area to place your audio file later.

6. Type a title for this audio slide. Figure 6.4 shows a slide prepared for an audio file.

6.4 A placeholder slide prepared for an audio file.

7. If you want to place an image, such as a photograph of you making this recording, place it on this slide now.

8. Repeat the preceding steps for all other audio files you want to add.

9. Save your file.

Creating the Portfolio PDF File

Up until this point, you have a done a lot of prep work. Finally, the moment you've been waiting for has arrived. You are ready to turn the PowerPoint file into a PDF.

Step by Step

1. If necessary, start PowerPoint and open your PowerPoint portfolio file.

2. Go to File > Page Setup, choose Orientation > Slides, select landscape view, and click OK.

3. Go to File > Print and from the pull-down menu, select Adobe PDF as the Printer. From the Print What option box, select Slides.

4. Click on OK, navigate to your PDFs folder, and then click on Save. You may need to wait a few minutes while the PowerPoint file is converted to a PDF file. Close PowerPoint.

5. Start Acrobat Professional and open the PDF you just created.

6. When you open your PDF, you may find that each of your slides contains a white border, as shown in Figure 6.5. If you want to remove the border, you have two options for removing, or cropping it. (To *crop* means to select the part of the image you want to retain and delete the rest.)

   - For a simple way to crop, go to Document > Crop Pages. Click on the Margin Controls > Remove White Margins and Page Range > All. Click OK. Acrobat crops at the margins.

   - To specify an exact crop, use the Crop tool. To begin, click on the Crop tool in the toolbar to select it (or go to Tools > Advanced Editing > Crop). Decide where you want to crop and then in one corner of the slide, click where you want to begin the crop and then drag to the diagonally opposite corner where you want the cropping to end. With the area now defined, click inside the rectangular selection you created. From the window that pops up, select Crop Margins > Crop and then under Page Range, select All, as shown in Figure 6.6. Click OK.

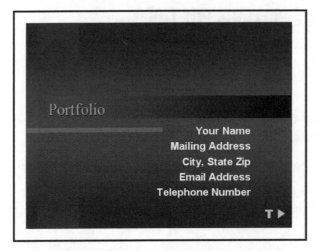

6.5 If your PDF file has a white border that you want to remove, use the Crop tool to remove it.

6.6 Select Remove White Margins from Crop Margins and Page Range All.

7. When the cropping process is complete, save the file as
Portfolio.pdf in your Portfolio Files folder.

8. Save your work.

These pages may take time to create, but they give your portfolio interactivity and depth. A resume can say what your skills and abilities are, but
these links to samples can deeply enrich the viewers' understanding by
showing them examples of your successes.

In This Chapter

In this chapter you took the JPEG images you created of your work and inserted them into slides at the end of your presentation. You also created placeholder slides that will later contain your audio and video samples. Finally, you turned your PowerPoint presentation into a PDF by using Acrobat Professional. In the next chapter, you will add your multimedia files to your PDF.

6.1 Idea Starters

Directions: Take a moment to reflect on the following questions and then write an answer to each.

1. How do you want people to view your multimedia files? Describe their experience.

_____

_____

2. After you answer question 1, determine whether the preparation in this chapter matched your idea. If so, why or why not?

_____

_____

3. Look through your PDF portfolio. Are there areas that you wish were better or different? If yes, describe those areas here.

_____

_____

4. Are there areas of your portfolio that you can change before you continue to the next step? If so, how will you change them?

_____

_____

continued

continued

6.1 Idea Starters

5. Are you starting to plan to collect new and more kinds of artifacts from now on about the work you do? What kinds?

_____

_____

Add Multimedia Files

In This Chapter

- Examine the difference between attaching and embedding files
- Add video files to your PDF
- Add audio files to your PDF
- Create a button for viewers to play your audio files

One of the capabilities of Acrobat that makes it attractive for producing portfolios is for PDFs to link to and contain multimedia files. When we say multimedia, we mean that you're combining video, audio, and animation files into your presentation. The only limitation for placing multimedia in PDFs is that the multimedia file must be in a format that Acrobat recognizes. In addition, the viewer will need to have the free Windows Media Player installed to view the files.

For this book, we have been recommending that audio, video, and animation multimedia files be saved in the AVI format. This format is primarily used by Windows computers, but the players are also available for Macs. The one exception is Flash files, which is a format that Acrobat recognizes. Therefore, it's unnecessary to convert these files.

Attaching Files Versus Embedding Them

In order to properly set up your PDF so that others can view your work, you need to understand the difference between attaching a file to your PDF and embedding a file within the PDF. A file that is *attached* to a PDF document is linked to it and has to travel with the PDF file when you copy it to a disc (or distribute it) if it is to work properly.

Any file that is *embedded* becomes part of the PDF and does not need to travel with the PDF when you move it or send it for review. Embedded JPEG, video, and audio files are copied into the PDF document. In the previous chapter, the JPEG images you added to your presentation were embedded files.

Managing and Attaching Multimedia Files to the PDF Portfolio

Before you begin adding multimedia to your PDF portfolio file, be sure that the location in which your are saving your work contains both a Portfolio Files folder and a Multimedia folder. Next, if you haven't done so already, move all of the AVI (video and audio) and SWF (Flash animation) files from your Artifacts folder to the Multimedia folder, as shown in Figure 7.1. These are the multimedia files you will be placing on the portfolio pages.

7.1 The Multimedia folder contains audio, video, and Flash animation.

Adding a Video File

To begin, you will add the video files to your PDF. In the next section, you will add your audio files.

Step by Step

1. Start Acrobat Professional and open your PDF portfolio file.

2. Click on the Pages tab so that you can see thumbnails of your port-folio pages.

3. Set up your view so that you can see several of the portfolio pages in Pages view and at the same time see the selected slide at a view large enough to read the text, as shown in Figure 7.2. To do this, click and drag the bar between the Pages view area and the main window to the right to allow as many thumbnails of pages as possible to be seen. Size the view of your main window by going to View > Fit Page or by using the Numeric Size window in the tool-bar to Fit Page.

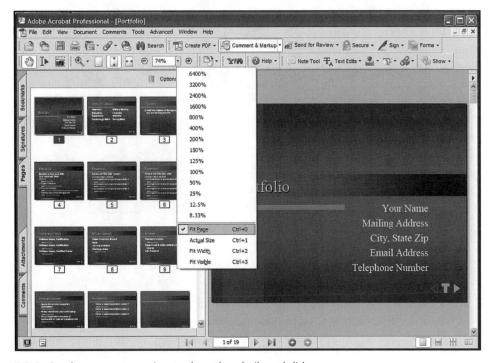

7.2 In Acrobat, set up your view to show thumbails and slides.

4. Go to the first placeholder slide you created to hold your video files.

5. Select the Movie tool by clicking on it (see Figure 7.3). You can display this toolbar by going to Tools > Advanced Editing > Movie Tool.

7.3 The Movie tool.

6. When you select the Movie tool, the cursor turns to crosshairs. On the first placeholder slide for your video sample, click and drag a box in the area where you would like to see the video play, as shown in Figure 7.4. Acrobat will then prompt you to locate the video file and make choices about how to play it by displaying the Add Movie dialog box.

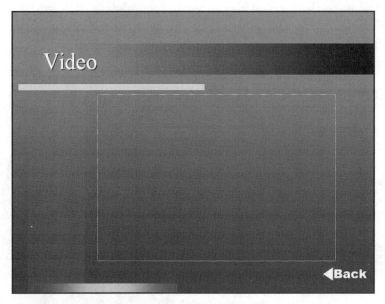

7.4 Draw a box in the location you want your video to play.

7. In the Add Movie dialog box, click on Browse, navigate to your Multimedia folder, and then highlight the video file you want to add. Click on Select. In the Add Movie dialog box, make the following selections:

- Choose Acrobat 6 (and later) Compatible Media.

- Click on both the Snap to content proportions and Embed content in document buttons.

- For Poster Settings, select Retrieve poster from movie. A *poster* is the first frame you see when you enter a PDF page with a video.

Your dialog box should now match the one shown in Figure 7.5

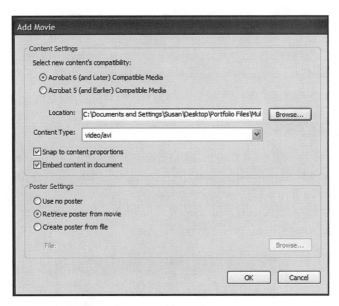

7.5 Select your movie file preferences.

8. Click on OK. Acrobat will place your video file on the page. The file will display with a red border as long as the Movie tool is active (see Figure 7.6), which means that you can move the video elsewhere on the slide or make changes to it. If necessary, move the video rectangle into position on the slide.

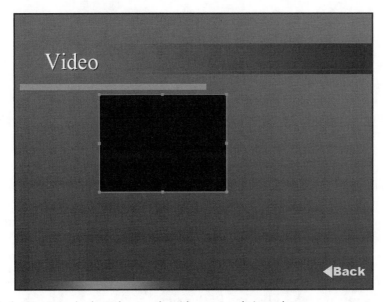

7.6 With the Movie tool selected, move the video rectangle into place.

9. Save your work.

Now you will set up how your video looks and plays. As you will see in the next Step by Step section, you have several options.

Step by Step

1. With the Movie tool selected, double-click within the video that you just placed. Acrobat displays the Multimedia Properties dialog box shown in Figure 7.7, which is what you will use to set up your video. In the next steps, you will use all three tabs (Settings, Appearance, and Actions) to set up your video.

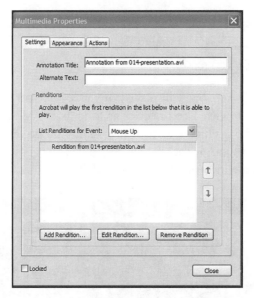

7.7 The Multimedia Properties dialog box gives you several options for how the movie looks and plays.

2. In the Multimedia Properties dialog box, click on the Settings tab. Under Renditions, click on the Rendition that contains your filename and then choose when you want the video to play, as shown in Figure 7.8. For example, you can choose Mouse Up so that the video plays automatically when a viewer enters the page.

For additional settings for this video, click on Edit Rendition. You can select to have video controls show or to play in a floating window rather than within the PDF page.

These are all personal design decisions. Experiment with them to find the settings you like best, or you can choose to leave them at their defaults.

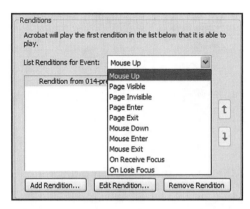

7.8 Determine when you want the video to play. In this case, the video is set to play when the viewer first enters the page.

3. While still in the Multimedia Properties dialog box, click on the Appearance tab. Here, you can change the border type, width, color, and style on your video, as shown in Figure 7.9. Notice the options under each category. For example, the options for the type of border are visible or invisible. If you prefer, you can also change the poster option from your original when you place the video file.

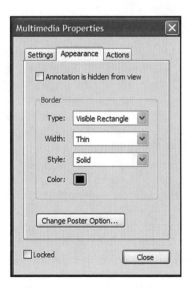

7.9 The Appearance preferences allow you to choose the video border and set the poster options.

4. Click on the Actions tab, but for now, leave all options as is (see Figure 7.10). If you later decide that you want to experiment with the video behaviors, the Actions area is where you can do it.

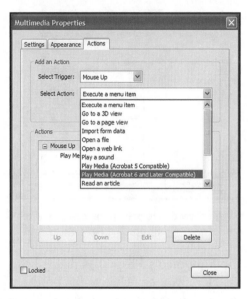

7.10 The Actions area gives you the opportunity to set even more options for the way that the video file plays.

5. In the Multimedia Properties dialog box, click on Close to set all your video options.

6. Switch to the Hand tool by clicking on its icon on the toolbar. Click on the video box to test the video playback. You will notice that the red border around the video frame disappears as soon as you click on the Hand tool. To edit the video settings again, click on the Movie tool again (the red border reappears).

Get Creative with Buttons

If you want to get really creative, you can use the Button tool to create a button to start and stop multimedia files. This tool is especially helpful if you place more than one video file on a page. The viewers can use a button to choose which video they want to watch first.

7. Repeat this step for any remaining videos you want to add.

Adding a Sound File

Although you can place a variety of different sound file formats on PDF pages, remember we are using the AVI format to simplify the video and audio production of the portfolio. We are also using the AVI format for both video and audio to ensure that the files use a common player for the viewer.

Although there is more than one way to make an audio file play, in this book you will embed the audio file in the PDF and then create a button that viewers can click on to play it. The method you use to embed an audio file is similar to the method you use to embed a video file.

Step by Step

1. Using the Movie tool (Tools > Advanced Editing > Movie Tool), embed the audio file as a small rectangle in a corner of the page. From the pop-up screen, browse to locate your audio AVI file.

2. With the Movie tool still selected, double-click the audio file box you just created.

3. In the Multimedia Properties dialog box, click on the Appearance tab. Under Border, select Invisible Rectangle as the Type.

4. Click on the Change Poster Option button and then select No poster. By setting the option to No poster, the rectangular border will display only when the Movie tool is active. You are making a Rendition of the audio file, but will place it out of the way (make it invisible) and instead create a button that viewers can use to play the sound.

5. In the Multimedia Properties dialog box, click on OK. Your page should now look similar to the one shown in Figure 7.11.

   Now that you have added the audio file, you can create the button to play the file.

6. Using the Button tool on the Advanced Editing toolbar, draw a rectangle on the page where you would like to create a button to play the audio file. The Button Properties dialog box displays, providing options for setting up that button.

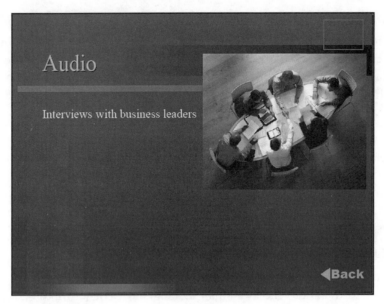

7.11 Place the audio AVI file into a corner of the page.

7. In the Button Properties dialog box, click on the Appearance tab. Choose a color for your button, a border if you want one, and the typeface and size of the text on the button, as shown in Figure 7.12. Do not close the dialog box.

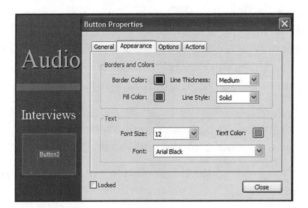

7.12 Setting the appearance of the audio button.

8. Click on the Options tab. In the Label field, type the word(s) that you want to appear on the button. As shown in Figure 7.13, this example uses the text "Play Audio." As long as the Button tool is selected, you may not yet see the text you have just typed.

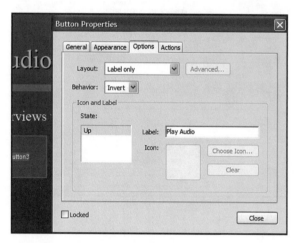

7.13 Adding the text you want to appear on the button.

9. Click on the Actions tab, and then under the Select Action drop-down menu, choose Play Media. (See Figure 7.14.) Click on Add to pick the file you want to play when the button is clicked. Choose the audio file that was placed in the corner of that page and then click on Close.

10. When you return to the view of your page, verify that the button is formatted as you intended, as shown in Figure 7.15.

11. Select the Hand tool so that you can clearly see the button label you typed. With the Hand tool selected, test the button and play the audio file.

12. Repeat this step for any remaining audio files you want to add.

13. Save your work.

Adding video and audio to your portfolio is fun and easy—and makes the portfolio even more interesting to view.

7.14 Adding the file you want to play.

7.15 Making sure the button displays properly.

In This Chapter

In this chapter you added video and audio files to your PDF. You also set up the appearance of these files in your PDF and created a button with which to play your audio files. In the next chapter, you will add links for your work samples.

7.1 Idea Starters

Directions: Take a moment to reflect on the following questions and then write an answer to each.

1. What value do you find in having video or animation available in your digital portfolio?

   _____

   _____

2. Can you think of more video samples you might want to collect in the future to demonstrate your special skills and abilities?

   _____

   _____

3. What value do you find in having audio available in your digital portfolio?

   _____

   _____

4. Can you think of more audio samples you might like to collect in the future to show your skills and abilities?

   _____

   _____

5. Can you think of a reason why a potential employer might be impressed seeing that you can create rich multimedia files that can be easily distributed?

   _____

   _____

Assemble the PDF Pages into the Portfolio

In This Chapter

- Create page-to-page links
- Create links to open new PDF documents
- Create links to start programs
- Fix linking errors

Now that you have all of the JPEG and multimedia files attached to your PDF pages, the next step of assembly is to link the PDF pages and the PDF samples to the portfolio pages. We will demonstrate this process using the example pages that we've used in the previous chapters.

Adding Navigation to Your Portfolio

Because not every portfolio will be read sequentially from page one to the end, you need to create a way for viewers to navigate within your portfolio. To do this, you use a series of links between pages.

For example, your Education page might include the name of your school and the dates you attended. Further, your page might contain text that lets viewers know that a copy of your transcript is available for review. So that viewers can easily view that transcript, you might turn that descriptive text into a link so that when viewers click the text, they are taken to the page that contains your transcript. Then, you might provide a back button so that viewers can easily return to the Education page.

In the following sections, you will create several types of links in your portfolio PDF. You will

- Create a link between all PDF pages within your portfolio

- Create a link to open a sample of your work in PDF format, with a link to return to the portfolio PDF

- Create a link to another page in the portfolio PDF and back again

- Add a button to open a sample of your work in another program, such as Microsoft Word

- Add links to your table of contents page

To begin, you will link all of your PDF pages.

Creating a Link Between All PDF Pages Within the Portfolio

If your pages have graphical navigation, you need to create page-to-page links in Acrobat. (You do not need to do this if your portfolio uses text navigation and can instead skip to the next section.) Each forward arrow, back arrow, and table of contents (or home) link on each page needs to be linked.

Although this step may be a time consuming, it is what gives your viewers the ability to move around your portfolio as they wish rather than having to move through the pages sequentially. By adding this interactivity, you can improve the viewer's experience while also demonstrating your technical abilities.

Step by Step

1. Open your portfolio PDF and display the first page, your cover. Be sure the Pages pane displays, and set the view of the main page zoomed to fit.

2. Select the Link tool. (If the Link tool does not display in your toolbar, go to Tools > Advanced Editing > Link Tool.)

3. On the first page, locate your forward arrow graphic and then click and drag a box around it.

4. In the Create Link dialog box, under Link Action, click to select Go to a page view (see Figure 8.1). Currently, you are on Page 1, so you want the forward arrow to take you to Page 2. Click Next.

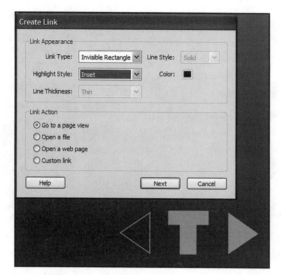

8.1 Creating a link within the PDF document.

5. In the Create Go To View dialog box, click on the destination page for the link in the Pages pane. In this case, you want to click on page 2. Click on Set Link.

6. When you return to your PDF page, you will find a red box indicating that it is an active link.

7. With the Link tool still active, double-click within the red box to open the Link Properties dialog box.

8. In the Link Properties dialog box, click the Appearance tab and choose the Link Style of Invisible Rectangle and the Highlight Style you prefer.

9. Click the Actions tab and confirm that the link will move the viewer to the page you want, in this case Page 2 (see Figure 8.2). Click Close.

10. Continue throughout the document, making a hyperlink for each navigation arrow and table of contents (or home) navigation graphic. Instead of repeating the preceding steps for each link you want to create, however, you can copy the navigation set you just created and paste it on each page of the portfolio.

11. Select the Link tool, if it is not already selected, and Shift-select each of the links around the graphics, one at a time.

Note

To see the page you are on, check the Pages area or the Control bar.

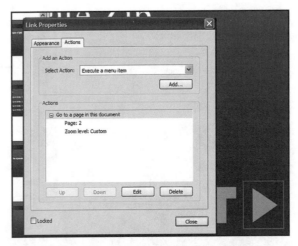

8.2 The Link Properties window shows that the link will move the viewer to Page 2.

12. Go to File > Copy, as shown in Figure 8.3.

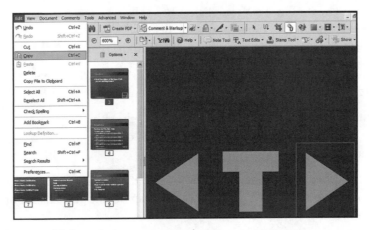

8.3 Copy the created links so that you can paste them to a new page.

13. Move to the next page and go to File > Paste, as shown in Figure 8.4.

14. With the Link tool still active, drag the copied link boxes into position around the navigation graphics on the new page.

15. Double-click on each link box to open the Link Properties dialog box.

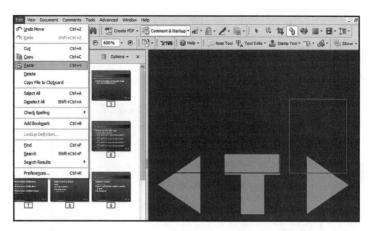

8.4 Paste the created links to another page. Be sure to edit each link's page properties to reflect the new page.

16. Click on Edit to change the new page destination number for that page. The link around the Table of Contents (or Home) navigation graphic will always remain the same.

17. Repeat steps 13–16 to paste the navigation set and update the link for each remaining link.

18. Save your work.

Now that you have added links to your navigation, you can add your additional PDF samples and then begin linking to both samples of your work contained within and outside of your portfolio.

Adding PDF Samples to the Portfolio

Likely, you now have several samples that are in PDF format. In this section, you will add these samples to your portfolio.

Step by Step

1. Start Acrobat Professional and open the Portfolio PDF in your Portfolio Files folder.

2. Set up your workspace so that you can see as many of the thumbnail pages as possible in the Pages pane. Set up the Main window to view the selected portfolio page by using the Fit Page command.

Note

Do not select the portfolio PDF you have open—a PDF file cannot be inserted into itself.

3. To add PDF pages to the portfolio PDF, go to Document >Insert Pages. In the Select File to Insert dialog box, navigate to the PDFs folder. Shift-select all of the items you want to attach to the portfolio (see Figure 8.5).

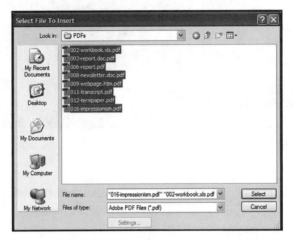

8.5 Use Shift-select to bring all of the PDF samples into the PDF portfolio document at once.

4. Select Location > After and Page > Last to insert the documents at the end of the portfolio PDF. Click OK. When you return to your portfolio PDF document, you should see the added pages at the end of the line of thumbnails in the Pages window (see Figure 8.6).

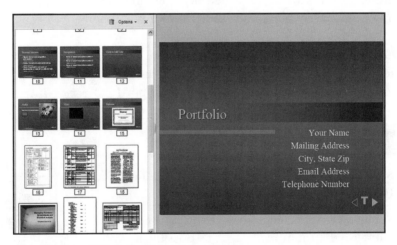

8.6 You will see the new PDFs in the Pages area.

5. Save your work.

Linking to a PDF Document Within the PDF Portfolio

For any samples you have that are included as PDF pages in your portfolio, you will need to create a link from the page that contains the description of the item to the actual PDF page of the item. In the following example, will we create a link from the word "Transcript" on the Education page to the actual PDF transcript that appears later in the portfolio. You can use this method to create links to all of your PDF pages.

Step by Step

1. In the description section of your portfolio, go to the first slide that contains a description that you want to turn into a link to the item's PDF page later in the portfolio.

2. Select the Link tool. If the Link tool is not already visible in your toolbar, go to Tools > Advanced Editing > Link Tool to find it, as shown in Figure 8.7.

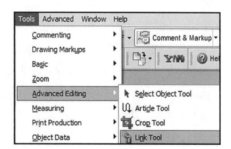

8.7 The Link tool.

3. Click and drag a box around the word you want to turn into a link. In this example, the word is "Transcript". If you prefer, you can also create a link from a graphic.

4. In the Link Properties dialog box that displays, click the Actions tab, and from the Select Action drop-down menu, select Go to a page view (see Figure 8.8).

8.8 Use the Link Properties dialog box to create links from your text or graphics.

5. Click Next and the Create Go To View window opens. Do not click on anything in the Go To View window yet.

6. Look over at the Pages pane. Scroll to the PDF you want to link to and select it, in this case the Transcript.

7. Go back to the Create Go To View window and click on Set Link.

8. Return to your PDF page. Around the word that you're linking from, notice that a rectangle displays, indicating the link you just made around the word, as shown in Figure 8.9.

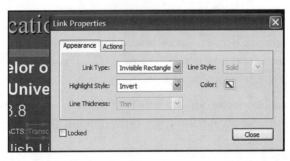

8.9 When you return to the portfolio page, a box displays around the newly linked word.

9. To format how the new link looks and behaves, with the Link tool still selected, double-click on the red rectangle. The Link Properties dialog box opens, as shown in Figure 8.10.

8.10 To edit an action (behavior), highlight the action and click on the Edit button.

10. To change the size of the linked page that appears on the screen, adjust the Zoom by going to the Actions tab, highlighting the action, and clicking the Edit button. In this example, the Transcript page is set to open to Fit Visible, as shown in Figure 8.11. Click OK.

8.11 To adjust how a linked page appears on the screen, adjust zoom.

11. When you return to the PDF page, select the Hand tool and click to test the new link. See Figure 8.12.

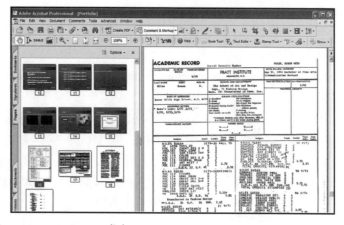

8.12 Don't forget to test your new link.

Fixing Broken Links

For directions on how to fix links that don't work properly, see the section "Correcting Linking Errors" at the end of this chapter.

12. Repeat the preceding steps for any other text or graphics from which you want to create links.

13. Save your work.

In this example, we used the word Transcript to create a link from the description to the actual transcript PDF page. In the next section, we create a button on the transcript PDF page to return viewers to the description page.

Creating a Button on a PDF Page

Every time you link to an example PDF from a descriptive page of the portfolio, it is important to give viewers an easy way to return to that portfolio page. One way to do that is to create a Back button. Your button could use words, a symbol, a single letter, or a graphic that contains a hyperlink back to the portfolio page. In the following example, you will create a button by using the Button tool.

Step by Step

1. In the Pages pane, locate the first sample page that needs a Back button. Click on it to bring that page into the main view.

2. Select the Button tool from the toolbar. (If the Button tool does not display, go to Tools > Advanced Editing > Forms > Button Tool.)

3. Click and drag a box to begin the creation of your button on the PDF page.

4. In the Button Properties dialog box, click the Appearance tab to begin "designing" your button. Set the border, color, and typeface.

   For this button we chose to make the Fill Color blue with no border around the button. We chose 12 pt. Helvetica Bold as the typeface and set the color to Black, as shown in Figure 8.13. Be sure to select a type size and color that is legible.

8.13 Use Button properties to enhance the appearance of your buttons.

5. Click the Options tab to set the action, or behavior, of how the viewer will interact with the button. See Figure 8.14.

We chose the Behavior of Push from the pull-down menu and typed in the text that would appear on the button (Return to Portfolio).

8.14 The Button properties options.

6. Click the Actions tab. Choose Go to a page view and then click on Add.

7. Click Next and the Create Go To View window opens. Do not click on anything in the Go To View window yet.

8. Look over at the Pages pane. Scroll to the portfolio page you want to link back to and select it—in this case, the Education page.

9. Go back to the Create Go To View window and click on Set Link. Click OK.

10. On the PDF page, locate the new button, as shown in Figure 8.15. If you need to move the button, change the color, or adjust the size of it, perform these changes with the Button tool selected.

8.15 The finished button.

11. After the button is complete, select the Hand tool and test the button.

12. Repeat the preceding steps for any other text or graphics you want to create links from.

13. Save your work.

Linking to a PDF Page Within the Portfolio

The process of creating links between descriptions in the portfolio and the pages that contain the samples is the same as creating links from descriptions to PDF Artifact Documents. The difference is in how you go back to the description page from the artifact page. To return to the description page from this kind of page, you will create links by using graphic navigation on each page.

This demonstration will be from the Education page to a page where an sample was placed on a Blank PDF portfolio page (such as the diploma, audio, and video files). We will create a return link from that sample portfolio page back to the description page by using the graphic navigation that was created on each page that contains a sample.

Step by Step

If you recall, we made a JPEG of the diploma and placed it on a Blank page, so there is a page in the portfolio for it already. Using the Education page again as an example, the description we will make into a link is the diploma description.

1. Go to the page on which you want to create a link.

2. With the Link tool selected, click and drag a box around the word you want to link from—in this case, "Diploma."

3. In the Create Link dialog box that pops up, select Link Action > Go to a page view.

4. Click Next. The Create Go To View dialog box will open.

5. Go to the Pages pane to the left of the workspace, scroll to the PDF page on which the diploma JPEG was placed, and select it. Using the Pages view lets you set the page number of the sample.

6. Go back to the Create Go to View dialog box and click on Set Link (see Figure 8.16).

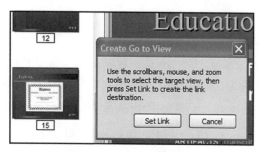

8.16 Create a link to the diploma artifact page in the portfolio.

7. Double-click the red link box to launch the Link Properties dialog so that you can format the appearance of the link, as shown in Figure 8.17.

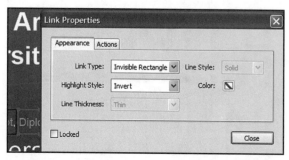

8.17 Using Link Properties to format the appearance of the link.

8. When the link is formatted, change to the Hand tool and test the link.

9. Save your work.

Creating a Back Link for the Graphic Navigation on the PDF Page

Now that you have a link to the sample (diploma) page, you need to turn the graphic navigation on the sample page into a link that returns viewers to the portfolio page with the diploma description.

Step by Step

1. Go to the Pages pane and click on the sample page so that it shows in the main window. Again in this example, we are using the diploma demonstration page.

2. Select the Link tool.

3. With the crosshairs, click and drag a box around the navigation graphic, in this case the back arrow and word "BACK."

4. Select Link Action > Go to Page View.

5. Choose the appearance of the link and click Next.

6. In the Pages pane, select the description page with the link to the sample (diploma)—in this case page 4, the Education page. See Figure 8.18.

8.18 Setting the page destination of the new link.

7. Go to the Create Go To View window and click on Set Link.

8. Switch to the Hand tool and test the completed button (see Figure 8.19).

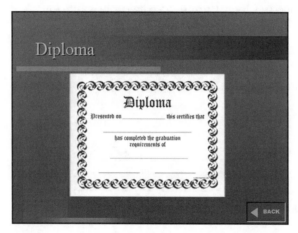

8.19 When you return to the sample PDF, switch to the Hand tool and test the link.

9. Save your work.

Creating a Link to Launch Another PDF Document in a New Window

In this section you will learn how to create a link on the PDF page that takes viewers to another PDF document. In this example, we will link the Education PDF page we having been using. The link will be to a sample that is a PowerPoint presentation. When clicked, this link will go to another PDF document and open it, rather than link to another page within the PDF document.

Step by Step

1. In the Pages pane, click on the page on which you want to create the link. In this example, we are using the Education page.

2. Select the Link tool and drag a rectangle around the words to be linked. For this PowerPoint sample, we are linking all of the words of description: "Term Project, A PowerPoint Presentation on Impressionism."

3. In the Create Link dialog box, choose Open a file, click on Next, and then click on Browse.

4. Navigate to the PDFs folder and select the PowerPoint PDF file. Click OK.

5. In the Specify Open Preference dialog box, choose New Window (see Figure 8.20) and click OK.

8.20 Set the preferences to open a new PDF window.

6. Format the look of your link when you return to the PDF by double-clicking on the red link rectangle.

7. When you are finished, change to the Hand tool and test your link. The PDF PowerPoint should launch in a new window on top of the Portfolio PDF.

8. Save your work.

When the viewer is finished, he or she can close the presentation and return to the portfolio, which is still running in the background.

Creating a Button to Launch a Word Document

Because many employers carefully review resumes, it is a good idea to offer a downloadable version of your resume in addition to the resume you include in your portfolio. This downloadable should be in the traditional resume format and should be saved as a Microsoft Word document. This way, you could leave this download as well as a hard copy with potential employers.

The following steps show you how to place a resume download button on the portfolio's Table of Contents page, but you can put a download button anywhere you feel one belongs in your portfolio.

Step by Step

1. In Acrobat Professional, go to your Table of Contents page (or other location where you want to add a download button).

2. Click on the Button tool and then click and drag a rectangle where you would like to place the resume download button.

3. In the Button Properties dialog box that displays, click the Appearance tab and set the size of the button type, the color of the button background, and the words that will appear on the button, as shown in Figure 8.21. (For more information about how to do this, see Chapter 7, "Add Multimedia Files." In this example, the button text is "Launch Resume as Word Document." As long as the Button tool is active, your text may not display on your button.

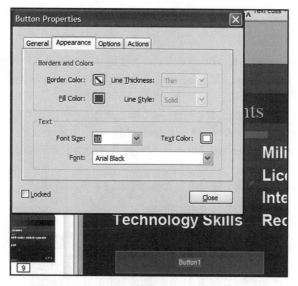

8.21 Formatting the appearance of the download button.

4. Click the Actions tab, and then from the Select Action drop-down list, click Open a file.

5. Click on Add, navigate to the Attached Files folder and highlight the Microsoft Word version (.doc) of your resume document (see Figure 8.22). Choose Select and then close the Button Properties window.

8.22 The Button Properties dialog box with Open a file parameters set to launch a Word document.

6. When you return to the portfolio page, the new button will appear, as shown in Figure 8.23. Select the Hand tool and then click on the new link to test it. When you click on it, Microsoft Word should start and the resume.doc file should open from your Artifacts folder. If the viewer does not have Microsoft Word installed on his computer, an error will display when the link is clicked.

8.23 The Table of Contents page with completed button to launch a Word document of the resume.

7. Save your work.

Linking the Table of Contents

Using the same link creation procedures as you did for linking your samples and pages within the PDF document, go to your Table of Contents page and create a link around each section to link to the first page of that section (see Figure 8.24).

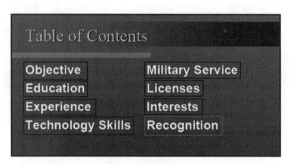

8.24 Table of Contents with hyperlinks being created for each section.

If you haven't done so already, be sure to test the links you've created. In fact, if you haven't already tested all of your new links, now is a good time to do so. If you find that you have links that don't work as you expect them to, the following section should be quite useful.

Correcting Linking Errors

If you test a link and the link goes to an incorrect page, you'll need to correct the link. This is a relatively simple fix.

Step by Step

1. Select the Link tool and double-click on the link that has the error.

2. In the dialog box that displays, click on the Actions tab.

3. Select the Action by highlighting it and click on Edit.

4. Type the correct page number.

5. Click OK and Close.

6. Switch to the Hand tool and test the revised link.

When you have all your links in working order, you're ready to proceed to the next chapter.

In This Chapter

In this chapter you created links so that viewers could easily navigate your presentation and your samples. You created links that linked to other pages in the PDF, links that opened new PDF documents, and links that started new programs, such as Microsoft Word. Also, you tested your newly created links to make sure they worked properly. In the next chapter, you will spend some time streamlining the PDF you have created.

8.1 Idea Starters

Directions: Take a moment to reflect on the following questions and then write an answer to each.

1. What are the advantages of including navigational links in your presentation?

   _____

   _____

2. What are the advantages of creating links that open new PDF documents or new programs, such as Microsoft Word?

   _____

   _____

3. Can you think of at least two reasons to test all of your portfolio links?

   _____

   _____

4. What are some of the consequences of sending a portfolio that contains links that don't work properly?

   _____

   _____

5. When you tested your links, did you find any links that were broken? If so, how many did you find and were you able to fix them?

_____

_____

Optimize the PDF Portfolio

In This Chapter

- Explore what it means to optimize a file
- Reduce the overall file size of your PDF
- Set up your portfolio so that it opens in full screen view
- Test the PDF portfolio to make sure it works properly

Just as you take care in selecting the words and images that describe you in your portfolio, you want to streamline the size of your portfolio and make sure it opens properly. To do this, you will optimize your portfolio.

Optimizing the PDF

In everyday language, to *optimize* something means to make it as perfect or effective as possible. In working with computers, however, this word takes on the additional meaning of increasing the speed and efficiency of the hardware, software, or file and reducing the size of files.

In order to send the best PDF possible to reviewers, you will need to optimize it, and this chapter shows you how. When optimizing the PDF portfolio, you have several areas to tune up:

- Metadata, or file image
- File size, which you want to reduce
- Preferences, such as how the portfolio is viewed

Adding Metadata

Metadata is information about a file that is contained with the file but invisible to the viewer (that is, it does not appear on the pages of images and text). Metadata, which often consists of key terms by which you can search for the document, is information that is accessible to the user and makes the document retrievable in a database.

Step by Step

1. Open the portfolio PDF document.

2. Go to File > Document Properties and in the Document Properties dialog box, click the Description tab.

3. Under the Description area, fill in as many fields as possible, paying special attention to the Keywords field. You can use Figure 9.1 as an example.

   The text that you enter in the Title field will be the text that appears in the title bar of the presentation page.

   The rest of the information will not appear in the document. However, the information will travel with your document and can be retrieved by others who want to know the details of the production and ownership of the portfolio, including the author's name or the version of Acrobat used to create the file.

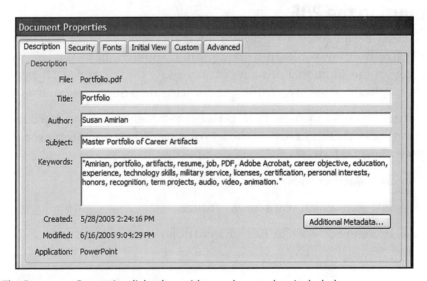

9.1 The Document Properties dialog box with sample metadata included.

4. Click OK to close the dialog box and add the metadata.

5. Save your work and close the portfolio PDF.

6. If you have any PDFs that are linked to the portfolio, repeat the preceding steps for each PDF.

Reducing the File Size

Because portfolios are often distributed electronically, you want your file size to be as small as possible. In this section, you will learn how to reduce the file size so that it runs efficiently from various storage media while showing your work in as much detail as possible. You have already done this to a degree in how you have structured and formatted the file so far. However, there are additional steps you can take now to make the PDF portfolio file even smaller, which will make it load quickly and move from page to page without stalling. To complete this step, you will need to make a duplicate of the portfolio PDF file.

Step by Step

1. Highlight the portfolio icon in the Portfolio Files folder and right-click on the icon.

2. Select Copy from the contextual menu.

3. Click anywhere in the white empty space of the folder and right-click again. Select Paste.

4. Right-click on the portfolio copy file icon and select Rename from the contextual menu.

5. Name the copy of the portfolio PDF Portfolio-small.pdf.

6. Open the new Portfolio-small PDF file.

7. Go to File > Reduce File Size and then choose the Acrobat 6 and later option.

8. Click OK and navigate to the portfolio folder where you will let the file copy over the duplicate of the master portfolio, named Portfolio-small.pdf. You can watch the progress bar at the bottom of the portfolio interface as it works to compress and reduce the file.

9. When the update is complete, save your work and close the file.

10. Compare the difference in the size of the original file with the size of the optimized file. In Windows, open the folder that contains these files and then go to View > Details. Make a mental note of the file size of each. See Figure 9.2.

Portfolio.ppt	79 KB
Portfolio.pdf	13,162 KB
Portfolio-small.pdf	11,706 KB

9.2 After you optimize your portfolio, you should see a difference between the master portfolio PDF file size and that of the optimized portfolio PDF file.

Setting the PDF Document Preferences

Ideally, you want your digital portfolio to capture the viewer's full attention. One way to do that is to set up your portfolio so that when it opens, it fills the viewer's entire screen. In this section, you will set up your portfolio to run at full screen.

One final way to optimize your file is to set up the preferences for how the file will work when the viewer explores the portfolio. You don't want viewers to see the Adobe Reader interface of toolbars and menus. Instead, you want to create a seamless interface, free of all unnecessary software. You will set the preferences so that files linked to your portfolio view properly when called by the links in the portfolio document.

Step by Step

1. Start Acrobat and open the PDF portfolio file.

2. Go to File > Document Properties or press Ctrl+D.

3. In the Document Properties dialog box, click the Initial View tab.

4. Although you can certainly make other choices within these document parameters, your portfolio will likely run best with the preferences shown in Figure 9.3. After you make changes to the settings, click OK.

5. Save your work.

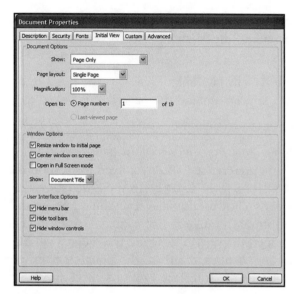

9.3 Set your portfolio preferences to match those shown here.

6. If you have any PDFs that are linked to the portfolio, such as JPEGs that you saved as PDFs in order to retain detail, repeat the preceding steps for each PDF.

With your PDF optimized, you can now test it to make sure it opens and works properly.

Note

To return to the Document Properties dialog box when menus do not display, press Ctrl+D.

Testing Your PDF Portfolio

There's nothing that will make you look less employable than a portfolio that doesn't work as it should. So to be on the safe side, you should test your PDF thoroughly to make sure it works just as you expect it to.

Step by Step

1. If necessary, start Acrobat and open your PDF portfolio file.

2. Test every link in the portfolio to make sure that it links to the item you expect it to.

3. If you have any attached PDFs, test each of those links also.

4. If you have any links that require a separate program to launch, such as the link to the Microsoft Word version of your resume, test these links.

5. Make a note of any bad links, as well as the number of the page that the link appears on and the page that is linked to.

6. Make any necessary changes.

   If you need to make changes to your portfolio PDF or if you want to change any preferences, you may need to turn on the display of your menus. If so, press Ctrl+D. In the Document Properties dialog box that opens, click the Initial View tab and under the User Interface Options, remove the checkmarks from the check boxes. When you open the portfolio again, the menus will display. After you make your changes, return to the Document Properties dialog box and re-check the Interface Options check boxes.

7. Re-test any broken links and make any final corrections.

8. Save your work.

Congratulations! You have just finished creating your master portfolio.

. . . .

Backing Up Your Work

Don't lose all of the time and hard work that you've put into creating your portfolio. If you haven't already done so, make a backup of this file by copying it to your hard drive, a USB flash drive, or other storage device.

. . . .

In This Chapter

You started this chapter by exploring what it means to optimize a file and then you optimized your own PDF portfolio to increase its efficiency and reduce its file size. You also set up your portfolio so that when it is opened, the presentation takes up the entire height and width of the viewer's screen. Finally, you tested each of the links in your portfolio to make sure they worked properly.

9.1 Idea Starters

Directions: Take a moment to reflect on the following questions and then write an answer to each.

1. What changes did you notice about your PDF file after you optimized it?

   _____

   _____

2. What have you learned from optimizing your PDF portfolio that you can apply the next time you create a PDF?

   _____

   _____

3. Can you think of additional metadata that would be beneficial to add to your PDF?

   _____

   _____

4. Are there other ways that you could optimize your PDF?

   _____

   _____

5. Does your portfolio PDF run smoothly? If not, propose ways in which you could troubleshoot problems and make corrections.

   _____

   _____

Manage the Portfolio Files

In This Chapter

- Make copies of the files you will distribute

- Back up and store your files

- Maintain your files and create a list of contents

A career portfolio can be an ongoing process. If your work requires yearly reviews, the portfolio may be a continuous project that is updated at least once a year. Job-hunting, promotions, and career advancement of any kind might benefit from having an up-to-date portfolio ready to show. One way to be ready is to make it as easy as possible to find your samples. As in the beginning of this process, file management at this end stage is key.

Putting Your Directory Structure to Work for You

Let's take a moment to review the file structure you've created up to this point. On your computer or the storage device you are using, you should have a Portfolio Files folder. Within that folder you should have three files: a portfolio PowerPoint, a portfolio PDF, and an optimized portfolio PDF. The four subfolders—Attached Files, Multimedia Files, PDFs, and Portfolio Artifacts—contain digital copies of the various items you used to create your portfolio. Take a moment to compare your folder structure with the one shown in Figure 10.1.

10.1 The Portfolio Files folder with subfolders, a PowerPoint presentation, and two PDFs.

Duplicating the Files Required for Distribution

When you get ready to send your portfolio, you don't need to send every digital file you've created up to this point. Instead, you will send only the optimized portfolio PDF and the files that are attached to it (it's not necessary to send embedded files).

In preparing for the distribution of your portfolio, the first step is to duplicate just the files that will go on the CD or other distribution media. Our recommendation is to always duplicate files rather than move the original file. This way, you always leave the master portfolio file folder intact, with all of your original and production files should you ever need to go to back to them.

Step by Step

1. Create a new folder on your computer (or the storage device you are using) and name it **Final Portfolio**.

2. Go back to your Portfolio Files folder.

3. Locate the optimized final portfolio PDF (Portfolio-small.pdf), right-click on it, and then select Copy.

4. Return to the Final Portfolio folder, right-click it, and then select Paste to place a copy of the optimized final portfolio PDF into the folder.

5. Repeat this procedure for the Attached Files folder. Right-click on the Attached Files folder, click Copy, and then return to the Final Portfolio Folder. Right-click and then click Paste.

The optimized portfolio PDF and the Attached Files folder should be the only files that need to be moved from the original folder structure to the Final Portfolio folder.

The multimedia files are embedded in the PDF portfolio so none of those need to be moved. The PDF pages were imported into the portfolio document, except for the PowerPoint presentation PDF. The Attached Files folder contains the only additional files that need to travel with the portfolio PDF—those documents that are linked to the PDF but not embedded within it.

10.2 The Attached Files folder.

Backing Up and Storing the Portfolio Files

The collection and storage of all of your digital files over time can require some planning and even investment. Plan for a storage method that has the largest capacity you think you might need and can afford. It is also helpful if the storage device is portable and easily accessible. Smart, long-term storage for your work should be

- Permanent (not on a rewritable media or protected from accidental deletion or overwriting)
- Redundant (more than one copy made)

This way, if anything goes wrong, you will have a backup and won't have to start over from the beginning.

Video or other multimedia requires more storage space than simple text documents. If you are serious about building your portfolio and you can afford it, consider purchasing a portable external drive just for storing your portfolio files. Our demonstration folder contains only a few items and takes up less than 1 GB of space. Already, these few items are too large for permanent storage on a Zip disk or a CD. You will want to make duplicate backups of your portfolio files and can use smaller media by splitting up the files among a number of CDs or DVDs, for example. If your primary storage drive fails, you want to have another backup.

Maintaining File Naming and Logs

To make it easy to work with your portfolio files as they grow in number, be sure to keep up your file naming and numbering by updating the "Creating a List of Portfolio Items" worksheet you started in Chapter 2. Having a list like this makes it easy to search for files, organize them, and retrieve them. You don't want to have to open 100 documents to see what is in each one the next time you are updating your portfolio.

Also, you might want to consider taking the next step and actually make a visual database of your samples. You can do this with programs such as Microsoft Office Access, FileMaker Pro, or specialized visual databases such as Extensis Portfolio. Visual databases allow you to search and sort your files by word or numeric identifications, as well as by thumbnail view and metadata. You could also use Adobe Photoshop Elements, which is easy to use and has a great photo organization feature.

Dealing with File Corruption, Viruses, and Other Data Disasters

It happens to everyone at some point in their digital lives—an important file becomes corrupt or is destroyed by a virus. If you have a backup, you can delete the bad file and replace it with a good one. If the file is not available, there are several strategies for attempting recovery:

- Professional help. This is often the most expensive but also the most direct and effective route to file recovery. Data recovery companies specialize in bringing digital files back to life. They can sometimes even recover files that have been erased from your computer.

- Data recovery software. Although you can purchase software that you can run on your computer to recover lost or damaged files, we recommed that—unless you know exactly what you're doing—you seek the help of a professional.

Making a List of Your Computer's Contents

It is often helpful to have a hard copy list of the contents of a drive or backup disc. This information tells you what is on a disc without your having to start up the computer or open the disc. A contents list can also give you information about file sizes and last dates of revision for each file. Keeping a hard copy of the contents of a disc with the disc can make it easy to search for files.

For a quick contents list, Windows users can make a screen capture of the file window (be sure to change to Details view) and then print the image. Also, by using programs such as Screen Print 32, you can select to capture a portion of the screen (for example, the contents of a directory window) and then print it to paper. A final option is to purchase third-party software that allows the contents of file windows to be printed directly to paper by using the Print command.

Keeping a Notebook

One way to keep all of the elements of your portfolio under control is by using a three-ring binder. Hard copies of Worksheet 2.2 will give you the number of each sample and a description of each file. Also, you can add sleeves to hold the CDs or DVDs with backups of the files, with printouts of the contents of each disc to make it easy to locate files.

In This Chapter

In this chapter you verified that you had a working directory structure, and you made copies of your optimized portfolio and the files that will be distributed with it. Additionally, you learned the importance of creating backup copies of you work and how to both maintain and update your files.

10.1 Idea Starters

Directions: Take a moment to reflect on the following questions and then write an answer to each.

1. Can you think of at least three consequences of not having back-ups of your work?

   _____

   _____

2. Think about a time when you lost a digital file. Describe what happened and how long it took for you to re-create your work.

   _____

   _____

3. What are some ways in which you could keep your portfolio files up to date?

   _____

   _____

4. What kinds of files or folders could you use to organize new samples for your portfolio?

   _____

   _____

5. Can you think of future occasions for which it might be important to obtain samples so that you can update your portfolio?

   _____

   _____

Distribute the Portfolio

In This Chapter

- Identify the file size of your portfolio and attached files
- Explore media for distributing your portfolio
- Create a portfolio CD that starts automatically
- Design an insert for your CD case

Your master portfolio is complete, functioning perfectly, optimized, and backed up. All of your original portfolio items are safely stored and organized. You are now ready to place your portfolio on various media for distribution. In this book, you will use the most common medium—the CD-ROM—to create copies of your portfolio that you can distribute.

Determining the Size of Your Portfolio

In order to know what types of media you will be able to use for distributing your portfolio, you first need to find the amount of memory your portfolio—and any linked files—requires. Fortunately, Windows makes this easy.

Step by Step

1. Locate the Final Portfolio folder on your computer (or the storage device you are using).

2. On the folder name, right-click and select Properties.

3. In the Properties dialog box, locate the file size. In the example shown in Figure 11.1, the file size is 12.9 MB.

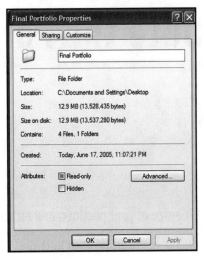

11.1 Use the Properties dialog box to determine the file size of your portfolio.

4. On a separate sheet of a paper, make a note of the file size and then click Cancel to close the dialog box.

Now that you know the file size, you can determine which methods of distribution are available to you.

Selecting a Distribution Medium

One of the first decisions you had to make when preparing to create your portfolio was to decide on a storage medium. Now that your portfolio is finished, you need to revisit the various types of media so that you can choose a way in which to distribute your portfolio.

The easiest method of distributing a portfolio is the common data CD. Most all computers have CD drives, which makes it highly likely that when you send your portfolio on a CD, the viewer will have the right equipment to run it. Also, because most computers come with CD burners, it should be relatively easy for you to create a CD.

Another advantage of distributing via a CD is that blank CD discs are relatively inexpensive and the capacity is adequate. CD capacity can be 650 MB or 700 MB. Check the labels carefully when you buy your blank CDs to make sure which capacity you are purchasing.

Although other media are available to distribute your portfolio, each has a limitation that CDs do not have. Table 11.1 lists common methods of distribution, as well as the advantages or disadvantages each may have.

Table 11.1 Common Ways to Distribute Your Portfolio

DISK TYPE	CAPACITY	COMMENTS
Floppy Disks	1.4 MB	Too small for most portfolios. Many newer PCs come without floppy drives.
Zip Disks	100, 250, or 750 MB	Adequate capacity, but drives are not commonly available in computers.
CDs	650–700 MB	Universally available and adequate capacity for most portfolios. This is the preferred method.
DVDs	4.7 GB	Excellent capacity, but formatting and hardware incompatibilities may limit access.

CDs stack up best when it comes to both the capacity to store large files and the capability to play in the average computer. In this book, we will show you how to burn a copy of your portfolio to CD and how to prepare the CD for distribution.

Creating the CD

The procedure for moving files from your computer to a blank CD and then creating (or burning) the CD varies depending on the operating system and CD software you are using. However, if you frequently create music CDs or make CD backups of your important files, you should find the following process to be familiar.

Step by Step

1. Locate your Final Portfolio folder. You will use the contents from this folder to create your portfolio CD.

2. Following the method recommended by your CD burning software, move the PDF portfolio file and the Attached Files folder to your CD. Be careful not to take the outer portfolio folder that holds the files on your desktop! You want the portfolio PDF file to be at the root level (or main directory) of the CD, as shown in Figure 11.2.

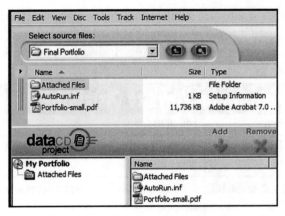

11.2 The Directory structure for your portfolio CD should have the portfolio PDF at the root level, not inside a folder.

3. If you want your CD to automatically start when placed in the CD drive of a PC, there is a small file that you can create and include when you burn your CD and that handles this function. If you prefer not to do this for some reason, skip to Step 8.

4. Start Notepad, which is a simple text-editing program that comes with Windows. Go to Start > Programs > Accessories > Notepad.

5. In the new document, type these two lines of text exactly as they are written—except you will replace the word *filename* with the name of your PDF file exactly as it appears in your Portfolio folder:

   [AutoRun]
   ShellExecute=filename.pdf

6. Go to File > Save. In the Save As dialog box, navigate to your Final Portfolio folder and in the File name box, type **AutoRun.inf**.

7. Move a copy of the AutoRun.inf file to the same place you moved the files to be burned to the CD. The AutoRun.inf file should be at the same root level of the CD as the portfolio PDF.

8. If you have not already been prompted to do so, name your CD. We suggest that you name your CD with your name and the word "portfolio"—for example, *Lastname_Portfolio.pdf*—for easy identification. (If the CD creation software doesn't prompt you for a CD name, you may have to look in the software Help to find out how to name it.)

11.3 Create the .inf file to make the portfolio CD run automatically when it is loaded onto Windows computers.

9. Burn the CD as directed by your CD-burning software. This may take a few minutes.

10. Remove the completed CD from the computer. Check to make sure that the CD runs by starting it from as many other computers as you can. If you added the auto-start capability, check that this works also. Otherwise, you risk sending a CD that no one can open.

Note

Mac users must open the CD and start the PDF by double-clicking on the PDF file.

Although you've accomplished quite a lot in this chapter, there's one last step: preparing an insert for your CD case and a label for the CD itself.

Designing Jewel Case Inserts and Labels

Jewel case inserts and CD labels make for a professional portfolio package and provide the finishing touches to your portfolio. Because the CD case, also known as the jewel case, will be one of the first introductions to your portfolio, it's important to think about the content and the design of the inserts and label (see Figure 11.4).

When you create your inserts and labels, be sure to include your name and full contact information on each—after all, there's no guarantee that the CD will remain with the CD case. If possible, design your insert in a way that complements the design of your portfolio and demonstrates your design sensibilities. For example, use the same color scheme and typefaces.

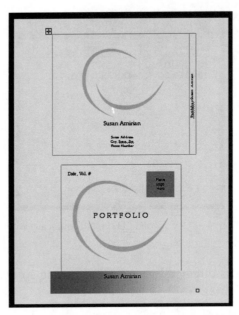

11.4 An Avery template for Microsoft Word includes graphics. You replace the text in the template and then print a professional-looking CD jewel case cover.

If you're lucky, your CD burning software may already include a built-in label maker program for creating inserts and labels. If it does not, however, you have several options for downloading templates from the Web. Both Microsoft.com and Avery.com provide free templates that you can use to design and create inserts and labels using Microsoft Word. Both sites also include step-by-step directions for downloading and using the templates. For more information, visit

- **Microsoft Office Templates homepage**
  Windows: office.microsoft.com/en-us/templates/default.aspx
  Macintosh: www.microsoft.com/mac/resources/
  templates.aspx?pid=templates

- **Avery pre-designed templates gallery**
  From the Avery.com homepage, go to Avery > Software > Pre-Designed Template Gallery > CD Cases/Emedia > Standard Jewel Case Inserts

In This Chapter

In this chapter you began by identifying the size of your portfolio and attached files so that you could determine what type of media would be available for distributing it. You then learned how to create a CD and add a Notepad file that would make the CD run automatically when inserted into the CD-ROM drive of a Windows computer. Finally, you explored options for designing CD case inserts and CD labels.

11.1 Idea Starters

Directions: Take a moment to reflect on the following questions and then write an answer to each.

1. Does your portfolio PDF fit on the storage medium you have chosen? If not, how would you go about solving this problem?

_____

_____

2. On how many different computers did you test your CD? Please describe the number and types of computers you used for testing.

_____

_____

3. What are the impressions that you want your CD insert and CD label to give viewers?

_____

_____

4. Do your CD insert and CD label send the impression you want them to? Why or why not?

_____

_____

5. Do you have additional information that would be useful to include on the CD insert and label? If so, please describe.

_____

_____

Print the Portfolio to Paper

In This Chapter

- Set up your portfolio for printing

- Print and organize your portfolio pages

- Explore ideas for presenting the paper version of your portfolio

A digital portfolio is designed to be shown on a computer screen. However, you will encounter different situations in which you might want to print your portfolio to paper. For example, you might want to have a document to hand your employer or to leave with a potential employer after an interview. Some employers prefer to have a paper copy for their file. If you are presenting the digital portfolio at a meeting, yearly review, or job interview, it's a good idea to have a printout as a precaution. That way, if anything goes wrong with the presentation of the digital file (the disc, the computer, or the power, for instance) you will be able to continue your presentation because you have a paper copy of your presentation to work with.

Choosing Your Paper

In spite of that design factor, most pages of the portfolio will print out nicely to paper—with some slight modifications to the document. Also, you will lose the linking function of the digital portfolio when you print it to paper, but you can still include the artifacts in a printout of the portfolio.

Because this is a portfolio, you may want to select a better quality paper than the traditional white office bond paper, just as you would if you were preparing a resume. Quality paper is especially important if you will be printing any pages in color. A slightly heavier paper or one with a texture or gloss could enhance the images.

Changing the Page Setup

By default, most programs are set up to print pages using *portrait orientation,* in which the page prints so that it is taller than it is wide. However, because your portfolio was designed to be viewed on a computer screen, your portfolio pages are set to follow the design of the computer screen—where the screen and pages are wider than they are tall, called *landscape orientation.*

Step by Step

1. Start Acrobat Professional and open your PDF portfolio file.

What to Do If Your Menus Don't Display

Because you opted to hide all of the menus for the final portfolio in the previous chapter, you may need to make your menus visible again. Press Ctrl+D to access the Display Properties dialog box, uncheck all of the User Interface Options, and click OK. Save the file, close it, and open it again in Adobe Acrobat Professional.

2. Go to File > Print Setup to access the Print Setup dialog box.

3. In the Paper box, use the Size pull-down menu to choose a paper size of Letter (8 1/2 inches by 11 inches), as shown in Figure 12.1.

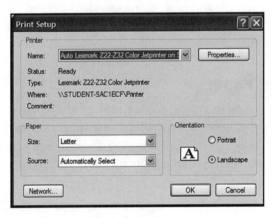

12.1 Use the Print Setup dialog box to select letter size paper.

4. In the Orientation box, select the Landscape (horizontal) option button so that the paper shape matches the shape of the portfolio pages.

5. Click OK to close the Print Setup dialog box.

After you set up your portfolio to print with a landscape orientation, you need to set up how your document will print.

Setting the Print Parameters

In this section, you will print your portfolio, but before you can do so, you need to set the printing preferences. By setting printing preferences, you can choose which pages to print or how many copies you want to print, for example.

Step by Step

1. Go to File > Print.

2. In the Print dialog box, select your printer by using the pull-down menu next to Name, as shown in Figure 12.2.

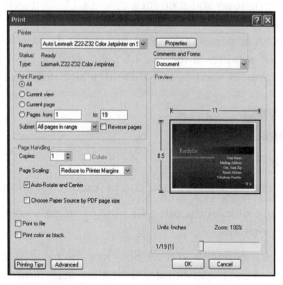

12.2 Use the Print dialog box to set up your document for printing.

3. Under Print Range, choose which pages you want to print.

4. Under Page Handling, set the number of Copies as 1. If you need to print multiple copies, it's often a good idea—especially for large documents—to first print a single copy to make sure everything prints as you expected.

5. Under Page Scaling, use the pull-down menu to select Reduce to Printer margins. Because most printers will not print all the way to the edge of the paper, making this selection reduces the file size to the safe area that your printer will print. This way you will not lose any part of your page in the areas unable to print. The page is reduced slightly overall and a white border will appear on each page.

6. Select Auto-Rotate and Center to position your portfolio in the center of the paper.

7. Click OK. Your file will be sent to the printer to print.

After your portfolio is printed, you can decide whether you want to print all of your samples.

Organizing Your Pages and Creating a Contents List

When printing, you might do a combination of printing out the main pages of the portfolio and then including a CD if viewers want to see your work samples. Alternatively, you could print everything and then organize the paper presentation into two parts: the portfolio pages and an appendix of samples at the end of the portfolio. If you opt to use an appendix, you might want to add a list of which items are included.

Step by Step

1. Open your PowerPoint file.

2. Duplicate the blank slide at the end of the presentation.

3. On the blank slide, add a title and a list of items you will include in the paper portfolio.

4. Using the drawing tools, draw a box over the navigation. Use the same color as the background to hide the navigation. When finished, your appendix page might look similar to Figure 12.3.

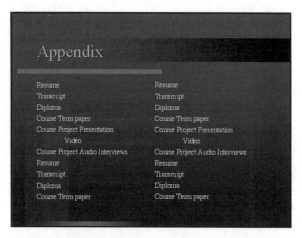

12.3 Create a contents list by going back to your portfolio PowerPoint.

Presenting the Paper Portfolio Document

So far, all you have is a collection of loose pages of your portfolio. However, to present a professional-looking package, it would be nice to bind the pages or place them in a folder in which the cover orientation matches the paper orientation. Although you might have to look harder, you can find binders and presentation cases that use the short side of the letter-sized paper. (These are available at office supply or stationary stores.)

One Last Thing!

Don't forget that in order to get to the menus to set up the document printing, you changed the PDF portfolio Document Properties. When you are finished printing, go back to the PDF file and return the settings to hide the menus the next time the portfolio opens. Go to File > Document Properties. Re-check all of the Hide options in the User interface Options (see Figure 12.4).

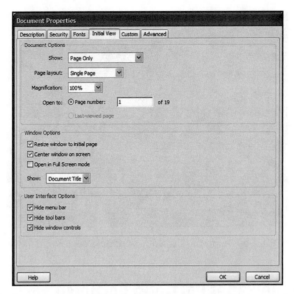

12.4 Don't forget to return the Document Properties to the settings before they were changed for printing the portfolio.

In This Chapter

In this chapter you set up your portfolio for printing by adjusting its page orientation to portrait and by reducing the page size so that the all of the contents would fit on a standard sheet of paper. After that, you printed and organized the pages, and you may have created an appendix page to list the contents of your samples. Finally, you explored ideas for presenting the paper version of your portfolio.

12.1 Idea Starters

Directions: Take a moment to reflect on the following questions and then write an answer to each.

1. Were there any pages that didn't print properly when you printed your portfolio? If so, please describe how you might fix these pages.

_____

_____

2. What are some of the benefits of having samples of your work appear in landscape and portrait orientations?

_____

_____

3. Can you think of other ways in which might be appropriate to print your portfolio (e.g. as a handout)?

_____

_____

4. Will you print your portfolio pages in black and white or color? Why?

_____

_____

5. What are the advantages and disadvantages of printing your portfolio in color?

_____

_____

Send the Portfolio for Review

In This Chapter

- Choose a method for sending your portfolio for review
- Learn to use Acrobat's commenting tools
- Get feedback about your portfolio before sending it for review

Before you send out your portfolio to potential employers, you want your portfolio to be in the best shape possible. Therefore, just as you did with your resume, it is a good idea to send out your master portfolio for feedback—from co-workers, teachers, friends, employment counselors, or colleagues, for instance.

Options for Receiving Feedback

The method you use to send your portfolio for review depends on the purpose of the review and the technical capabilities of the environment you are working in. For example, you could simply send out your portfolio and ask for verbal or written feedback. You can also use the commenting tools within Acrobat to get feedback within the document, at exactly the place where the comments are directed—on the page. Another option is to use an evaluation sheet to guide your evaluator to make sure that he or she considers all of the areas of the portfolio on which you would like to have feedback.

In this chapter, we will concentrate on the simplest, most universally available method of reviewing a document: using Acrobat. Acrobat provides a simple way to implement reviewing that can be used with very little coordination of computer systems or networks. Acrobat also offers a network system that can be part of a document review system within an organization or via the Internet.

Other Methods of Reviewing

First, a quick word about the review methods we will not be using: e-mail and browser-based reviews. E-mail reviews are discouraged because many e-mail systems limit attachments to 5 MB or fewer. Because you likely have many images in your portfolio, your PDF file could easily exceed this limit. Also, browser-based reviews can be difficult because they require that a Web server be set up for the review process.

If you want to try these methods on your own, or if your school or your company makes these methods possible, feel free to use them.

The Portfolio Review Process

We recommend sending a portfolio for review in two ways.

The simplest method to implement is to save your portfolio on rewritable media such as a rewritable CD or a Zip disk (if the reviewer has a CD burner or a Zip drive). If a rewritable disc is not available, however, a portfolio on CD could be copied to the desktop, reviewed, and then burned to another CD without too much extra time consumed. The reviewer can add notes and comments to the portfolio, save the changes, and send the file back to you by rewriting the disc or burning a new one.

The second way to distribute the portfolio for review is by putting the file onto a Web server. With a broadband connection and access to the Web server, the reviewer can download it to their desktop, review it, add comments, and return it to the server. Neither of these takes advantage of Acrobat's built-in tools to send files automatically, but you can use all of the editing and note-taking tools just as effectively.

How to Use Acrobat's Commenting Features

In this section, we provide a very brief overview of the Commenting tools in Adobe Acrobat and the ways in which you might use them in the portfolio creation process—or that others might use them in the review process. In Adobe Acrobat Standard and Adobe Acrobat Professional, these tools are built in. Reviewers using the free Adobe Reader, however, will need you to save your portfolio with comments enabled before sending the portfolio file to them for review. Because you may not know the software capability of your reviewer, you should enable comments every time you send your portfolio for review. To enable the comments feature, go to Comments > Enable.

Viewing Comments

Before you can begin reviewing or adding new comments, you need to see the comments. When your document contains comments placed by the Commenting tools, you can view them as a single, continuous list, as shown in Figure 13.1. To view comments, go to Comments > Show Comments List.

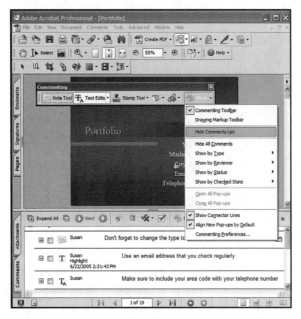

13.1 Use the comments list, shown at the bottom of screen, to view all comments in a document.

Adding Comments

You can find the Commenting tools in your Acrobat toolbar. If they do not display, go to Tools > Commenting > Show Commenting Toolbar.

These steps will bring the toolbar icons to your desktop. You can leave them as a freestanding toolbar or drag them to the menu at the top or side of the Acrobat workspace. Drag the toolbar using the separator bar at the left of each toolbar.

The Commenting tools consist of the following:

- **Note tool.** Notes are a good place to put reflective comments on a portfolio page, special instructions for viewing the page, or feedback from a reviewer, as shown in Figure 13.2. If more than one person is adding notes, each reviewer can select a different color or icon for his comments.

  To create a note, click on the Note tool and then click on your PDF page where you want to place the note. To move a note, simply drag it to a new location on your PDF page. To add your comment, double-click on the Note icon and in the pop-up note that opens, type in the white area of the note. To put your name on the note, right-click on the note and select Properties > General > Author. To change the Note icon and its color, select the Properties > Appearance menu.

13.2 Example of a note.

- **Text Edits tool.** This tool lets you select text and make edit indications on it such as striking it, adding a highlight, or underlining it. These are the traditional tools of someone who is looking at your portfolio as a proofreader.

  To use the Text Edits tool, first select Indicate Text Edits from the Commenting > Text Edit menu (see Figure 13.3). Next, select the letter, word, or group of words where you want to indicate an edit on the PDF page. Finally, select a specific editing feature from the Commenting > Text Edit list. If you are inserting text, an insert mark appears on the page at the insertion point, and a pop-up note opens where you can type the edits you want to make.

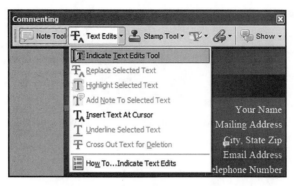

13.3 The Text Edits tool allows you to make edits directly in the text.

- **Highlight tool.** This tool functions just like the bright, fat markers you use to create highlights on paper or in textbooks. Select the Highlight Text tool from the Commenting toolbar and then click and drag it across any words on your PDF page, as shown in Figure 13.4.

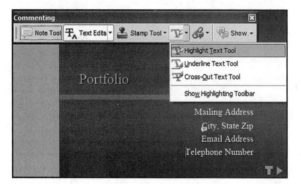

13.4 The Highlight tool menu.

- **Attach a File as a Comment.** This is an interesting set of tools—and very useful for portfolios. You can attach a file or even a sound that you can record by clicking on the Attach Sound tool button (see Figure 13.5). This allows you to add your personal commentary to samples of your work.

13.5 The Attach Sound tool lets you record and save small sound files and attach them to your artifacts.

- **Drawing Markups tools.** To display these tools on your desktop, go to Tools > Drawing Markups > Show Drawing Markups Toolbar, as shown Figure 13.6.

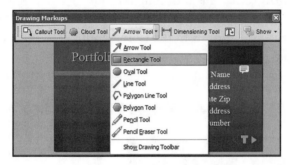

13.6 The Drawing Markups toolbar and tools.

- **Drawing tools.** You can use these tools to create designs on your pages, as shown in Figure 13.7. They are also attached to pop-up notes so that you can indicate a special area of the page you want to point out and then describe it in a text pop-up note. Right-click and choose Properties to change the color of the shapes. Like all of the Commenting tools, holding your mouse over the graphic pops up a ToolTip with the text of the note in it. To open the note, double-click on the graphic.

- **Text Box tool.** This tool allows you to create text on your PDF page. Click on the tool and then insert the cursor anywhere on your PDF page. To change the color of the box or border around the text, right-click on the text box and choose Properties. To change the size or font of the type in the text, go to View > Toolbars > Properties Toolbar. The Properties Toolbar changes depending on what is selected on the PDF page. Highlight the text in the text box, and the Properties Toolbar changes to Text Properties.

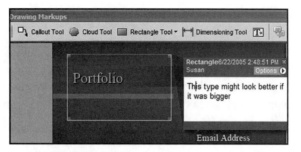

13.7 The Rectangle and Note tools in action.

- **Pencil tool.** The Pencil tool is a free drawing tool that will draw any shape you like. The pencil will show up in the Comments page. Although you cannot type in the drawing, you can add a pop-up notation by right-clicking and selecting Open Popup Note. You can also go to Comments > Show List and type in the Comments list area next to the icon. To access the typing area, click in the white space to the right of the Note icon in the list. As with the Drawing Tools, right-click in the drawing and choose Properties to change the color, thickness, and opacity of the pencil.

· ·
Putting the Commenting Tools to Work for You

For more help on using Acrobat's amazing Commenting tools, check out the Help menu.
· ·

In addition to having reviewers add comments to your PDF portfolio, it's helpful to give them guidance as to the type of feedback you want. One way to do this is to use an evaluation worksheet.

The Evaluation Worksheet

Regardless of which method you choose for receiving feedback about your portfolio, it's helpful to include an evaluation worksheet. The *evaluation worksheet* includes a definition of the expectations for the work so that the evaluator can judge whether—in his or her opinion—the work meets the specified criteria. In the case of a portfolio, the evaluation worksheet ensures that your evaluator considers the range of areas that you would like him or her to evaluate. This evaluation is important because you will use it to make improvements in your portfolio.

As an example, you can use the following evaluation worksheet for requesting feedback about your portfolio. Whenever you send your request for review, you can include this document to help direct the feedback and to also make the review process easier. The PDF of the evaluation worksheet employs the Commenting tools, described in this chapter, to place checkmarks in the boxes and add text comments to each category that is reviewed.

13.1 Portfolio Evaluation Worksheet

Evaluator: Please review the digital portfolio and then use this worksheet to rate its effectiveness in each of the following areas. For each item, please select Excellent, Satisfactory, or Needs Improvement. If you are using Acrobat to review the portfolio, drag a checkmark into the box before one rating in each area. Also, you may add specific feedback by double-clicking the note icon before the word "Comments."

Hardware/Software Mechanics

1. **Distribution media:** The CD or DVD runs and launches the portfolio program.

   ☐ Excellent   ☐ Satisfactory   ☐ Needs Improvement   ☐ Comments

2. **Portfolio program:** The portfolio PDF loads, starts, and runs efficiently.

   ☐ Excellent   ☐ Satisfactory   ☐ Needs Improvement   ☐ Comments

3. **Multimedia:** All audio, video, and animation within the portfolio plays properly.

   ☐ Excellent   ☐ Satisfactory   ☐ Needs Improvement   ☐ Comments

4. **Links:** All links are visually evident to the viewer, understandable, and work appropriately.

   ☐ Excellent   ☐ Satisfactory   ☐ Needs Improvement   ☐ Comments

Quality of the Presentation

5. **Overall visual appeal:** The portfolio has a professional look and feel, appropriate for the career path of the subject. The graphic look is visually consistent throughout the portfolio. The portfolio looks attractive and appealing on the screen, and all elements are easy to read and understand.

   ☐ Excellent   ☐ Satisfactory   ☐ Needs Improvement   ☐ Comments

6. **Navigation strategy:** The method of moving about the presentation is clear, intuitive, and professional. The placement of navigation is consistent throughout the portfolio. Every page has a clear way to get to the next page and to the home or contents page.

   ☐ Excellent   ☐ Satisfactory   ☐ Needs Improvement   ☐ Comments

7. **Usability:** The portfolio is presented in a logical order. The information is accurate and free of errors. The navigation is easy to see. Contact information is included.

   ☐ Excellent   ☐ Satisfactory   ☐ Needs Improvement   ☐ Comments

8. **Use of technology:** Portfolio plays on the computer with CD (or DVD) drive and Windows Media Player. Adobe Acrobat or Adobe Reader is the only installation that may be required. The viewer does not receive error messages when viewing the portfolio.

   ☐ Excellent   ☐ Satisfactory   ☐ Needs Improvement   ☐ Comments

9. **Organization/structure:** The subject headings and the order in which the portfolio content is presented are logical. Appropriate examples are associated with related text descriptions of experience or achievements.

   ☐ Excellent   ☐ Satisfactory   ☐ Needs Improvement   ☐ Comments

10. **Graphics:** Images are clear, appropriate, and of excellent quality.

    ☐ Excellent   ☐ Satisfactory   ☐ Needs Improvement   ☐ Comments

(continued)

(continued)

13.1 Portfolio Evaluation Worksheet

11. Captions: Captions set appropriate expectations for the images or links to which they are related.

☐ Excellent   ☐ Satisfactory   ☐ Needs Improvement   ☐ Comments

12. Multimedia: Multimedia is of professional quality and appropriate to the portfolio. It is clearly labeled and intuitive in how it is played.

☐ Excellent   ☐ Satisfactory   ☐ Needs Improvement   ☐ Comments

Content

13. Content choice: The education, experience, and achievements highlighted in the portfolio through text and examples are appropriate and professional.

☐ Excellent   ☐ Satisfactory   ☐ Needs Improvement   ☐ Comments

14. Effectively communicates experience and competencies: The education, experience, and achievements highlighted in the portfolio through text and examples provide an accurate understanding of the subject's true abilities.

☐ Excellent   ☐ Satisfactory   ☐ Needs Improvement   ☐ Comments

15. Demonstrates technology skills effectively: The preparation and presentation of the portfolio demonstrates an excellent level of skill in all aspects of creating a multimedia presentation using technologies—planning, organization, preparation, writing, graphics, audio, and video.

☐ Excellent   ☐ Satisfactory   ☐ Needs Improvement   ☐ Comments

Package

16. Disc: The disc is labeled professionally and clearly with the subject's contact information and date.

☐ Excellent   ☐ Satisfactory   ☐ Needs Improvement   ☐ Comments

17. Case: The package in which the disc is delivered is well designed and informative.

☐ Excellent   ☐ Satisfactory   ☐ Needs Improvement   ☐ Comments

18. Supplementary materials: Additional materials, such as print documents, are of professional quality and have been given the same thought and consideration as the portfolio.

☐ Excellent   ☐ Satisfactory   ☐ Needs Improvement   ☐ Comments

General Comments

_____

_____

_____

This portfolio was reviewed by:

_____

In This Chapter

In this chapter you chose a method for sending your portfolio for feedback. Also, you learned about using the various features in Acrobat for reviewing and commenting. Finally, you examined an evaluation form that you could use to direct the type of feedback you receive and to make the review process easier for the person evaluating the portfolio. In the next chapter, you learn how to prepare portfolios for special purposes and see examples of portfolios that others have created.

13.2 Idea Starters

Directions: Take a moment to reflect on the following items and then write an answer to each.

1. Please describe at least three advantages of getting feedback about your portfolio.

   _____

   _____

2. Please describe at least three disadvantages for not getting feedback about your portfolio.

   _____

   _____

3. Please list at least five people who could provide objective feedback about your portfolio. Describe your relationship to these people.

   _____

   _____

4. Are there any specific areas of your current portfolio that you expect reviewers will definitely comment on? Please describe.

   _____

   _____

5. Are there additional areas of feedback that you could add to the evaluation feedback worksheet? Please describe.

   _____

   _____

Special Purpose Portfolios

In This Chapter

- Examine the need for creating mini-portfolios
- Learn how to create different mini-portfolios
- Explore how to enhance the design of your portfolio

So far you have collected, constructed, stored, backed up, and reviewed your master portfolio—the demonstration of all of your many talents, skills, and achievements. Before we end, let's talk about special purpose portfolios. These are *mini-portfolios,* which you build from your master portfolio, that are targeted to a special audience or purpose. This chapter also shows you examples of portfolios in which students have taken their designs to the next level.

Creating Mini-Portfolios

In this chapter, you will see examples of and build the following mini-portfolios:

- E-mail: Designed to be small enough in size to travel through e-mail

- Course: Demonstrates skills and abilities acquired while taking a course

- Kiosk: Showcases non-interactive content that can be played as a running "video"

As already mentioned, when constructing each of these mini-portfolios, you first begin with your master portfolio. This is where the advantage of having a *digital* portfolio kicks in—you don't have to go back to your PowerPoint and start from scratch. Instead, you simply go back to your master portfolio and choose which pages you want to use in the mini-portfolio. Then, you can *extract* the pages, or pull them out, of the master portfolio and rearrange them to create the new, mini-portfolio. The following sections show you how to create each of these mini-portfolios in more detail.

The E-mail Portfolio

Today, many portfolios are sent via e-mail. But often, the file size of master portfolios are just too large for most e-mail systems to accept. In this case, you will want to have a special e-mail portfolio on hand so that you can take advantage of any opportunties that arise.

An *e-mail portfolio* is a mini-portfolio that shows just a few of your best accomplishments and work samples and is optimized to travel through an e-mail system. Because most e-mail systems limit users to a maximum size of 1 MB for a single e-mail, the target when building an e-mail portfolio is to keep the file size as far below 1 MB as possible while showing as much of your best work as possible.

Step by Step

1. Start Acrobat and open your master portfolio.

2. Go to Document > Extract Pages (see Figure 14.1).

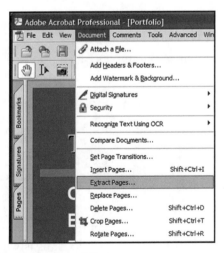

14.1 Extract pages from your master portfolio.

3. In the Extract Pages dialog box, enter the number(s) of the page(s) you want to extract (see Figure 14.2).

4. Click to select the Extract Pages As Separate Files option, also shown in Figure 14.2. You do not want to delete the pages when extracting—you want to leave your master portfolio intact.

5. Click OK.

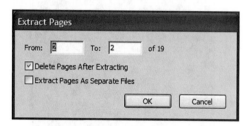

14.2 Do not delete the extracted page from your master portfolio.

6. Save the extracted pages into a new folder.

7. Assemble the extracted pages into a new mini-portfolio by going to File > Create PDF > From Multiple Files.

8. Navigate to the folder that contains the extracted PDFs and select the entire group by pressing Ctrl+A.

9. When the newly assembled PDF opens, use the Page window to click and drag the extracted pages into the order you want the pages to appear, as shown in Figure 14.3. A line will appear between the slides to indicate the new position of the page being dragged.

   Alternatively, in the selection window, put the extracted pages in the order you want them to appear.

10. When you save the new PDF file, it is called Binder by default. Rename your portfolio PDF.

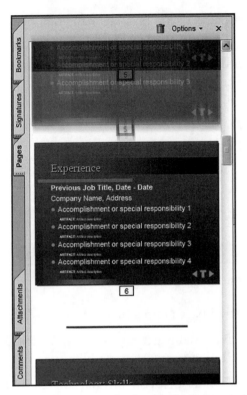

14.3 Click and drag page thumbnails to re-order them in the Pages window of any PDF document.

The Course Portfolio

Often, you can use examples of course work to demonstrate your new knowledge and proficiencies. Whenever you take a course, you can create a portfolio of the various exercises, research, products, projects, and presentations that comprised the course. By doing so, you are able to demonstrate the value of your education. A *course portfolio* contains examples of your accomplishments and abilities by showing work you have done for class. To target your work to a particular audience, you can add reflection about the assignments as text or audio notes.

The following sections show examples of course portfolios created by students just like you.

Course Portfolio Example #1: Al Pisacano

Al Pisacano created a course portfolio for his Imaging Technology course to showcase all of the research and assignments he produced during the semester. To begin, Al selected one of the default design templates in PowerPoint. Al then placed JPEGs of his graphics files on the PowerPoint slides. He placed text assignments as text boxes on the slides and used the Acrobat Notes tool to add comments about the process of completing each assignment. In the text assignment, Al referenced a Web site. He made the underlined the text of the Web address and changed the color in PowerPoint. Finally, in Acrobat, he used the Link tool to hyperlink the words so that when the viewer clicked on them, a Web browser would launch and take the viewer to the Web site.

14.4 An Imaging Technology portfolio by Al Pisacano.

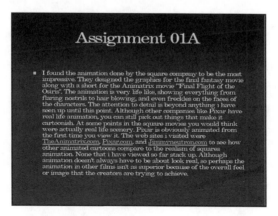

14.5 This portfolio showcases class assignments...

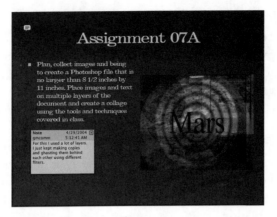

14.6 ...and Al's ability to work with various software.

Course Portfolio Example #2: Brian Christiaens

Brian Christiaens used PowerPoint slide designs to build his portfolio. He added the navigation in Acrobat as buttons with arrow icons to go Forward and Back. He created a button with a text label to go to the Table of Contents. Some of Brian's samples were placed on slides and made into PDFs. Other artifacts, like his resume, were linked to the PDF portfolio as an individual PDF artifact. Brian added a button on the bottom of the resume to return to the Table of Contents.

14.7 Brian Christiaens's course portfolio includes his resume...

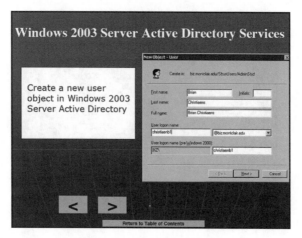

14.8 ...along with examples of skills learned during the course.

Course Portfolio Example #3: Kimberly Strow

Kimberly Strow created a course portfolio using PowerPoint and a slide design. After she placed her text and images on the slides in PowerPoint, she saved the slides as PDF files and then added Notes to her portfolio pages in Acrobat. Kimberly chose to use the Acrobat navigation to move viewers through her portfolio rather than create on-page graphic navigation or buttons. The fireworks Slide Design works well for a course portfolio, but is probably too informal a design for a career portfolio for most professions.

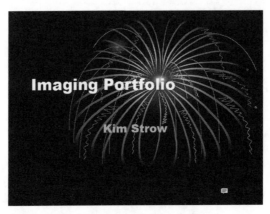

14.9 The opening slide from Kimberly Strow's course portfolio.

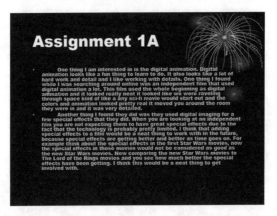

14.10 This slide shows evidence of Kimberly's critical thinking skills...

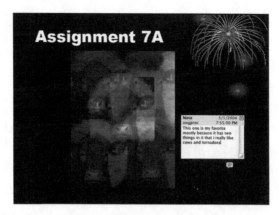

14.11 ...while this slide shows Kimberly's imaging and Acrobat skills.

Course Portfolio Example #4: Rick Hamlet

Rick Hamlet was an undergraduate student when he created this course portfolio for Imaging Technology. He used Keynote, the Apple presentation software, to create his templates and pages. Apple Keynote is very similar to Microsoft PowerPoint. Keynote offers attractive backgrounds and themes, including this notebook design that was perfectly suited to a portfolio presentation. Rick placed his text and graphics on each page in Keynote, then saved the presentation as a PDF file. He chose to use the Acrobat navigation to allow viewers to move through his portfolio.

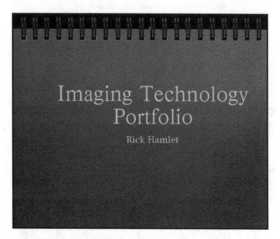

14.12 Rick Hamlet used Apple Keynote to create his presentation.

14.13 This slide shows Rick's creative side...

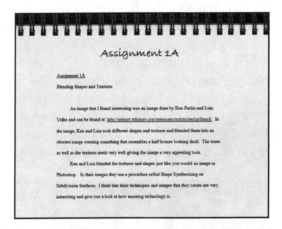

14.14 ...and this slide shows his writing skills. Notice the included hyperlink.

The Kiosk Portfolio

You can take any artifacts and pages from your master portfolio that do not require interaction and create a self-running kiosk-style presentation of your work. If you are giving a presentation, this could play in the background as the audience enters the room. It could play on a computer at a job fair.

Exploring Special Backgrounds and Design Templates

Now that you have created a portfolio using the design templates of Microsoft PowerPoint, you might be thinking about creating your own special design templates. The following sections show examples of design work that other students have done. In these course portfolios, students have created their own backgrounds and design themes using photo and paint programs such as Adobe Photoshop and drawing programs such as Adobe Illustrator.

Design Example #1: David Summers

David Summers created a portfolio of course work to demonstrate his accomplishments in Imaging Technology. David created his original backgrounds in Adobe Photoshop rather than using a PowerPoint template. He saved each page out of Photoshop as a PDF and then assembled the PDFs into a final PDF portfolio file.

For his page design, David chose to create a navigation menu along the left side of each page of the portfolio. This navigation design allowed viewers to go anywhere in the portfolio from any page. Because this is a course portfolio, the navigation is labeled by assignment number. David included text on the portfolio pages, including an introduction of himself. Because he is a skilled animator, David used Flash animation in his portfolio on the opening page. He demonstrated his construction of assignments by using the Print Screen feature to create screen captures, then labeled the graphics in Photoshop so the viewer could follow how he accomplished each assignment.

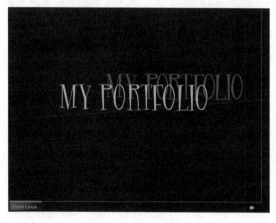

14.15 The opening page from David Summers's portfolio.

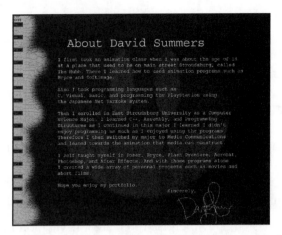

14.16 David created an effective introductory "letter" welcoming viewers to his portfolio.

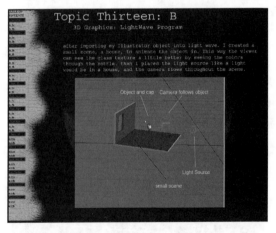

14.17 Note that this portfolio is a highly visual and contains an extensive navigation menu.

Design Example #2: Eleni Kikos

Eleni Kikos created a course portfolio that used the graphic metaphor of a film strip. You can see each frame is numbered, with two links at the bottom of each page. On the left side is a link to the Table of Contents, and on the right is a link to the next page. The navigation is subtle but clear, reinforces the film idea, and doesn't interfere with the viewer focusing on Eleni's artifacts. The checkmark at the top of the film is the link to the Notes created in Acrobat where Eleni recorded her reflections about each assignment. By using Acrobat's Notes properties, you can select the icon that appears on the page when a note is present but closed.

14.18 Eleni Kikos's opening page sets the theme.

14.19 Subsequent pages continue the theme...

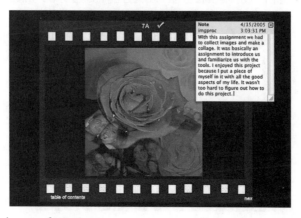

14.20 ...and include notes for reviewers.

Design Example #3: Gretchen Ragazzo

As a graduate student in the teacher education program, Gretchen Ragazzo created a course portfolio. She chose to use the metaphor of a book as the theme for her portfolio. For the background, Gretchen modified photographs of a book cover and its pages in Photoshop. She then placed the text and portfolio artifacts on the blank book pages in Photoshop and saved out each completed page as a PDF file. Gretchen designed her navigation by using a Table of Contents and included word links on each page to return. She also provided viewers with a "Next" link to view her portfolio one page spread at a time. On each page, Gretchen made reflective notes about her experiences performing the assignments by using Acrobat's Notes tool. In Acrobat Preferences, Full Screen Appearance, Gretchen chose the Background color of her PDF file to be black, creating the border around each of her portfolio pages when viewed at Full Screen.

14.21 The book theme invites viewers to enter Gretchen Ragazzo's portfolio.

14.22 A Table of Contents enables viewers to go directly to the section they are most interested in...

14.23 ...and special Next and Table of Contents links on each slide enable viewers to navigate easily.

Design Example #4: Jack Wrenn

Jack Wrenn used Photoshop to design a custom cover, Table of Contents, and page background for his course portfolio. He placed screen prints and text on the backgrounds and saved each page as a PDF that he then assembled into the final PDF portfolio file. Jack designed navigation that was consistent on each page of the portfolio and allowed viewers to go from any page to any page, including the Table of Contents. Jack used Acrobat's Note tool to place reflective comments about each assignment on the pages.

14.24 The opening screen in Jack Wrenn's presentation.

14.25 This portfolio includes an extensive Table of Contents.

14.26 By using consistent navigation, viewers can move from one page...

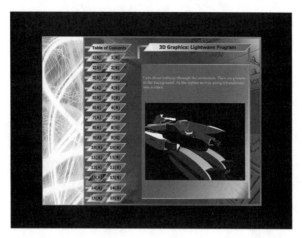

14.27 ...to any other page or the Table of Contents. In this way, the navigation doesn't interfere with the samples of Jack's work.

Design Example #5: Jenna Tress

Jenna Tress designed a creative and informal portfolio to showcase her work for the course Imaging Technology. She used a photograph of cork for the background. She placed each of her samples on the cork background in Photoshop and added graphics of pushpins and notes to complete the illusion. Jenna added Acrobat Notes for both the assignment descriptions and course reflection.

14.28 Jenna Tress used a corkboard background to create a bulletin board theme.

14.29 Although the artwork is imagery she created for a class...

14.30 ...the images provide evidence of her creative and technical abilities.

Design Example #6: Julian Napolitan

Julian Napolitan designed his course portfolio around the idea of a museum. He used a photograph of a museum as the first page, making a hyperlink around the door. When the viewer clicks the door or the word "Enter," the Table of Contents page displays. Inside, Julian placed each sample in a frame on a white background, paralleling the museum experience. He used simple text navigation to go to the Table of Contents or to the next page. The circle graphic in the middle of the bottom of each page is a link to open Notes that contains Julian's reflections on each assignment. Julian manipulated the photograph and created the frame background for each page in Photoshop.

14.31 The opening page for Julian Napolitan's portfolio.

14.32 The museum theme provides a consistent and familiar feel...

14.33 ...while also providing a way to showcase his work (by placing it in frames).

Design Example #7: Pat Wiencek

Pat Wiencek was a graduate student when she created this course portfolio to demonstrate each assignment she completed. Pat created a custom portfolio background in Adobe Illustrator. She placed the text and assignment graphics for each assignment on the blank background and saved each one as a PDF file. One thing that was unique and attractive about her portfolio design was that Pat created a front and back cover. On her interior pages, she used screen captures of the images to show each assignment. Instead of on-page graphic navigation, Pat used the Acrobat interface to allow viewers to move through her portfolio.

14.34 Pat Wiencek used Illustrator to create a personalized background.

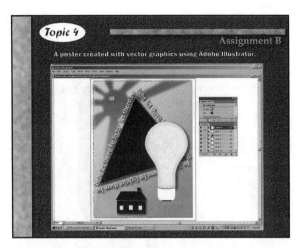

14.35 This background was carried through the sample portion...

14.36 ...and onto the specialized back cover.

Design Example #9: Tom Spitznas

In this last example, Tom Spitznas created a very professional course portfolio following the style of a Web site. The first page of his portfolio was designed like a Web site splash screen, or opening screen. When you launch the portfolio, a Flash animation plays with Tom's opening title and music. When the animation finished, the presentation automatically turns to the next page, his table of contents. Tom designed each page with a text menu so that viewers could get to any page in the site.

In addition, Tom included a navigation bar at the top of each page for what he decided were the most wanted destinations: Home, Table of Contents, and Contact.

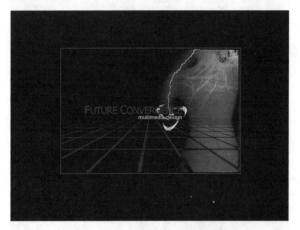

14.37 The opening screen of Tom Spitznas's portfolio is similar to a Web site splash screen.

14.38 This portfolio contains a combination of easy-to-read text...